D0779093

SHOW ME HOW TO
SHARE THE
GOSPEL

SHOW
ME
HOW
S·E·R·I·E·S

SHOW ME HOW TO
SHARE THE
GOSPEL

R. Larry Moyer

Kregel
Publications

Show Me How to Share the Gospel

Copyright © 1998 by R. Larry Moyer

Previously published as *Larry Moyer's How-To Book on Personal Evangelism*

Published in 1998 by Kregel Publications, a division of Kregel, Inc., P.O. Box 2607, Grand Rapids, MI 49501.

Library of Congress Cataloging-in-Publication Data
Moyer, R. Larry (Richard Larry).
    Larry Moyer's how-to book on personal evangelism / by R. Larry Moyer.
        p.   cm.
    1. Evangelistic work.   2. Witness bearing (Christianity)
    I. Title.
BV3790.M835   1998   248'.5—dc21   98-17621
                                                    CIP

ISBN 978-0-8254-3882-0

Printed in the United States of America

2 3 4 5 / 13 12

To David, my son,
who along with eternal life in Christ
and my dear wife,
has been an undeserved gift from God.
Thanks for being my "buddy"
and for those meaningful walks
and talks we have enjoyed together.
May you never lose your zest for life
and the Savior.

Table of Contents

Acknowledgments

ലൂ

I confess! Knowing where to start and stop in thanking the many people who have made this book possible absolutely bewilders me. As always, though, there are those who deserve special recognition.

A heartfelt thank you goes to the many brothers and sisters in Christ throughout the world who, as I have traveled in evangelism for over twenty-five years, have prayed for me, listened to me, and interacted with me. Because of the way God used your attentiveness and your feedback, my debt to you is enormous.

I am forever in debt to my dear wife, Tammy, whose foremost thought is always, What can I do for you? so I can be free to speak and to write. Why God would give me such an undeserved treasure, I have no earthly idea.

My thanks to Joy Kupp, who so patiently read my handwriting, typed and retyped the manuscript, and often did so despite my many interruptions about so many other items. Many thanks upon thanks. I was helped by your skills, but I was so deeply touched by your cheerful, servant spirit.

The feedback given me by Julie Boudreaux, Kathy Krach, Marsha Marlowe, and Linda Zach was tremendous. As readers, they could see things that were more difficult for me as to see. Thanks for reading the manuscript so carefully and responding with grace and truth.

Adria Ger's editing skills were invaluable. Thanks for pointing out those errors and details that only an editor often sees and explaining what I should have said and how I should have said it.

Thanks for being such gifted and godly servants and making so close to your heart what is so close to His—the reaching of the lost!

Introduction

If somebody introduced you to and offered to you the most reward-ing thing in life, would you take it?

"Of course," you answer, "I'd be a fool not to!"

You're right! And *that* is what makes evangelism not just enjoyable, but exhilarating! It *is* the most worthwhile thing in life.

Think about it! If God uses you in any way to introduce someone to Jesus Christ, your life has now counted for eternity. Somebody will not be separated from God as God used you to speak His name to them. Thanks to the working of God through you, they didn't get a better job, a bigger house, or a newer car. They received something so much bigger and eternal. Their eternal destiny was changed—and most likely the eternal destiny of the people closest to them because of the rippling effects of one person reaching another who reaches another who reaches another! No wonder the disciples had reason to get excited when He said, "Do not be afraid. From now on you will catch men" (Luke 5:10).

But look at the icing on the cake. What positively could be more exciting than being on assignment with the One who is on assignment with you? Doesn't the Great Commission conclude, "And lo, I am with you always"? Evangelism is partnering up with the Almighty. *He* has to bring the lost to Christ. We are only the instruments, not the power. But as we walk in faithful obedience to Him, scared to death but wanting to be used in evangelism, He's helping, comfort-ing, strengthening, encouraging, and teaching us. What He was when He saved me—a God of grace—He is in me to save others—a God of grace. God's desire is not to chastise us for when we blow it in evangelism, but always to help us learn from our mistakes, profit from them, and keep speaking His name. As He told His disciples, "Follow

Me, and I will make you fishers of men" (Matt. 4:19). To such a God of grace, I respond, "Lead on, I'll follow. Thanks for the privilege!"

My earnest hope is that what the God of grace has taught me in this book sets you free and causes you to say, "Hey, I can do this. By God's grace and with His help I am going to consistently talk to other people about Christ and clearly present the Gospel." If that happens, all the time spent in putting these thoughts together will be worth it all. And I cannot wait for that day when we are forever in His presence. You can introduce me to the people God used you to bring to Christ, and I'll introduce you to the people God used me to bring to Christ. Then together, we'll sing the "Hallelujah Chorus" in the presence of the King. What a day that will be to recognize afresh that we were participants and not mere spectators in the most rewarding thing in life!

Chapter One

How to Develop
an Evangelistic Lifestyle

Some time ago, I was speaking at a conference on evangelism. Near the end of the conference a man said to me, "I realize that evangelism shouldn't be merely a program or activity; it should be a way of life. But how do I make it that? How do I develop an evangelistic lifestyle?"

Anyone who wants his or her life to count for something eternal ought to ask the same question. How do I develop an evangelistic lifestyle? To receive the needed help in this area, we ought to ask, Is there anything about the lives and lifestyles of people in the New Testament that could help me develop an evangelistic lifestyle?

The answer is yes. As we study this topic, several things become clear.

We Must See People the Way God Sees Them

In Matthew 9:36, the observation is made concerning Christ, "But when He saw the multitudes, He was moved with compassion for them, because they were weary and scattered, like sheep having no shepherd." The New Testament speaks of Christ being moved or filled with pity eight times. He looked beyond people's faults and saw their need—they were like sheep without a shepherd.

Many times Christians feel that being around non-Christians is an unpleasant experience. Some unbelievers are very self-centered and their language can be less than desirable. We forget, though, that the problem is not what they do, it's who they are—individuals who have never met the Savior. As Christ looked beyond the person's actions and saw the problem, we are to do the same. We must have a heart of compassion toward non-Christians and see them the way Christ does. His practice is to be our pattern.

A number of years ago, several missionaries were killed by the Auca Indians in Ecuador. The father of one of the missionaries made the statement, "I feel sorrier for those poor Indians than I feel for my own son." That's a spirit of compassion!

We Must Give God Obedience, Not Excuses

The basis of evangelism is the Great Commission. Christ's command is: "Go into all the world and preach the gospel to every creature" (Mark 16:15). Luke 5:1–11 tells us about one of the first things Christ taught His disciples in evangelism. Using the metaphor of catching fish, He taught them to catch men. After they had fished an entire night with no success, Christ said to Peter, "Launch out into the deep and let down your nets for a catch." Any fisherman acquainted with the Sea of Galilee would understand that if you don't catch any fish at night, you might as well settle for no fish. Despite this fact, Peter answered, "Master, we have toiled all night and caught nothing; nevertheless at Your word I will let down the net." Miraculously they caught a net-breaking, boat-sinking load, and Jesus said, "Do not be afraid. From now on you will catch men." His message was simple: "When I say do it, *do it!*"

We sometimes think that we aren't called to speak to a lost neighbor about the Gospel because we may not be able to answer his or her questions. Sometimes this concern has some merit. At other times, it becomes an excuse behind which we hide. After all, Christ's calling is to us as well as to the first disciples, and He can provide the miraculous catch.

We Must Be People Who Pray

When we turn to the New Testament, we find that those who gave themselves wholeheartedly to evangelism also gave themselves to prayer. Not only did they plead *with* men for God, they also pleaded *for* men with God. We find them asking God for the opportunities to speak the Gospel (Col. 4:3). They also requested the courage they would need when they received that opportunity (Eph. 6:19). Although the emphasis is on believers praying for themselves and others who are evangelizing, they also interceded before God on behalf of the lost (1 Tim. 2:1–4).

Pray and keep praying. As you do, expect God to answer. Praying in faith is believing not only that He *can,* but also expecting that He *will.* A homemaker, after many years of praying, saw her alcoholic husband come to know the Lord. When asked how she prayed, she answered, "I prayed not only believing that God could save him, but also that He would." Should God in His sovereignty not answer such a prayer, we must respond appropriately, avoiding any kind of mental or verbal attacks on His character. But He wants us to pray knowing He can and expecting that He will.

We Must Make Contact

No one would dispute the fact that Jesus Christ had an evangelistic lifestyle. The amount of time He spent with sinners attests to this. He was even known as their friend (Matt. 11:19). We cannot have personal evangelism without personal contact. How can we regularly have contact with the lost? Several suggestions might be helpful. Our homes can provide an evangelistic outreach. We can entertain non-Christians for dinner or a backyard cookout, invite them to watch the Super Bowl with us, or come over for some homemade ice cream. Occasions such as these sometimes lead to informal discussions about spiritual things.

We can also take the opportunity to include them in things which interest us and may interest them. That might be a Friday night football game or an evening at the fair. It could be a fishing trip or a picnic by the shore. Events such as these convey to them that not only do we enjoy the Lord, we also enjoy life.

We should also do business with them. Believers can easily get into a rut. By that I mean we get our hair cut by Christian barbers, our cars repaired by Christian mechanics, and our homes built by Christian carpenters. There are times when that may be the wisest thing to do. But there are times when we don't give a non-Christian consideration simply because he or she is a non-Christian. As there are dishonest and unreliable Christians, there are honest and reliable unbelievers. Giving unbelievers our business can provide good contact for sharing the Gospel. The point is, make contact. Personal evangelism demands personal contact.

We Must Not Let Fear Stand in Our Way

In the New Testament, those who shared Christ with others were not people who never knew fear. Instead, they were individuals who allowed courage to overcome fear. Even in the face of persecution, they did not let fear stand in their way. In 1 Thessalonians 2:2, Paul says, "But even after we had suffered before and were spitefully treated at Philippi, as you know, we were bold in our God to speak to you the gospel of God in much conflict."

We will talk about the devastating problem of fear in a future chapter, but when we are faced with the possibility of persecution, the New Testament encourages us to do several things. First, just as the disciples did, ask God for boldness (Acts 4:29). Not only does God have a generous supply of physical blessings for His children, He also has a generous supply of boldness. Second, concentrate on the message (1 Thess. 2:3–4). When you know you have the truth, just as the disciples discovered, you cannot keep from speaking the truth (Acts 4:20). Third, have the proper motivation (1 Thess. 2:5–8). When you care, you must share. Commitment to people should result in conversation about Christ.

For the most part, we are fortunate in not being persecuted as the disciples were. We are usually simply afraid of losing a friend, being thought less of because we are Christians, being less popular in the neighborhood, or having doors slammed in our faces. Although the ramifications of this kind of rejection are not as great, courage is required.

Regardless of what we fear, we must not let fear stand in our way. We must be in command of it, instead of it being in command of us.

We Must Learn How to Share Christ

When we study the book of Acts carefully, it becomes clear that the disciples knew how to lead someone to Christ. Starting where the person was, they knew *how* to lead that person to saving faith in Christ as the Holy Spirit worked.

If we are going to have an evangelistic lifestyle, we, too, must know how to lead someone to Christ. In light of this, those who consistently evangelize have found it helpful to master a method. Obviously, one will have to adapt it to particular situations and people, but mastering a method makes most people more consistent in sharing Christ and more confident as they do so.

Whatever approach you use, make certain it makes the Gospel clear. The Gospel in its simplest terms is: Christ died for our sins; Christ arose from the dead (1 Cor. 15:3–4). Therefore, a good approach in sharing the Gospel should cover the basic doctrine of sin (so they understand their need), the death and resurrection of Christ (so they understand God's way of salvation), and faith (so they know what they need to do). It should also give non-Christians ample opportunity to interact with you so you can be sure they are following you and understand what you are saying. Two chapters from now we will discuss such a method.

Conclusion

One other thing needs to be said about developing an evangelistic lifestyle—*start now!* Someone has said, "True obedience does not procrastinate nor question." To have an evangelistic lifestyle demands involvement, not mere intention. The only way to become a golfer is by golfing. The only way to become a fisher of men is by fishing for men.

Evangelism is for you! God has chosen not only to bring lost people to Himself—He has also chosen to let you in on the blessing. The message hasn't been committed to angels but to you. In obedience to Him as His disciple, and in appreciation for His gift, follow the example of Peter, who said, "Master, we have toiled all night and caught nothing; nevertheless at Your word I will let down the net" (Luke 5:5). Start now!

QUESTIONS FOR REFLECTION

- When you are around non-Christians whose conduct or habits you may find annoying or even repulsive, what are some of the first thoughts you should entertain?

- What are some of the excuses you are prone to give God for not evangelizing as you should?

- What are some of the ways that come to mind whereby you can have meaningful contact with non-Christians?

- As you think about the fears the early disciples had in evangelism, what do you suppose went through their minds?

- As you think of past opportunities you may have had to share the Gospel and didn't, what could you have prayed for that would have helped?

Chapter Two

How to Turn a Conversation to Spiritual Things

"If individuals would just walk up to me and say, 'I want to talk about God,' I wouldn't have any difficulty talking about spiritual things with non-Christians. But I don't know how to bring up the subject when they don't." That sentiment and sometimes those exact words have been expressed to me by numerous individuals. One of the greatest frustrations in evangelism is how to turn a conversation from golf to God, or, in other words, from the secular to the spiritual.

That problem is intensified by the post-Christian era in which we are living where people have not come from the God-conscious background they did fifty years ago. The longer I have been in evangelism, the more people I have met who have never darkened the doors of a church.

To begin to get a handle on this area, several underlying facts have to be understood. When properly understood, these facts have a "freeing up" effect in evangelism. One begins to realize that turning a conversation to spiritual things is not as easy as it sounds but neither is it as hard as we are tempted to make it.

Fact #1—There Is No One Way to Do It

That's right! Instead, there are as many ways as there are people to whom you will speak. What believers often do is memorize five or more key words, phrases, or sentences to use in turning a conversation to spiritual things. It becomes a bit frustrating when they are in an actual situation and none of the five ways work. They then think to themselves, "How can I get the person to say what he was supposed to have said so I can ask what I was suppose to ask had he said what he was supposed to have said?" It's humorous to think about, but frustrating when it happens. Live with the comfort and the freedom of understanding there is no one way or even five ways to turn a conversation to spiritual things.

The Bible testifies to the fact that although we only have one message for the lost (Christ died for our sins and arose) there is no one way to introduce this message. Several examples of spiritual truth being shared are recorded, such as Jesus with Nicodemus in John 3 and with the Samaritan woman in John 4. In Acts 10, we read of Peter sharing the Gospel with Cornelius and in Acts 16, Paul shares the Good News with the jailer. None of these examples are recorded, however, with the purpose of telling us how to turn a conversation to spiritual things. Since people and their cultures differ, there is no one way to approach everybody on spiritual matters. If I'm speaking to a dairy farmer in my home state of Pennsylvania, I'll approach things differently than I would if I'm talking to a businessman in southern California.

Fact #2—Experience Is Essential

One can so easily approach this subject with the idea that when a person learns how to turn conversations, he or she will then know how to evangelize. Instead, just the opposite is true. *One learns how to turn conversations by evangelizing.* Those who turn conversations well do so because they evangelize often. Since they have this experience, they have built up a repertoire of possibilities. In any given conversation, they are able to reflect on what they have done or said in previous experiences that helped to move conversations in the right directions. So, as the previous chapter stressed, start evangelizing—*now!* Let God use your experience to teach you how to turn conversations to the spiritual.

Fact #3—Prayer Makes the Difference

One can know every way under the sun to turn a conversation, but if God does not provide the opportunity, it will never happen. Nor will it happen if one does not have the boldness to take advantage of the opportunity. Therefore, one needs to pray that God will provide both the opportunity and the boldness needed to speak when the opportunity is given. I can testify firsthand to how He works. Many, many times as I've asked Him for opportunities He has provided them.

Paul the apostle knew fear in evangelism. Otherwise, he would have never asked believers to pray that God would grant him boldness. He requests prayer in Ephesians 6:19 that "utterance may be given to me, that I may open my mouth boldly to make known the mystery of the gospel." He literally needed prayer that when he opened his mouth to speak the Gospel, it might come out boldly.

Fact #4—Hurriedness Can Hinder Witness

Often when we have difficulty turning conversations to spiritual things, it is because we are trying to move the conversation too fast. Depending on where the non-Christian is spiritually and the condition of what the Bible calls the "soil" in which the seed is about to be sown, it may take five minutes to turn a conversation to spiritual things or it may take five hours. Regardless, you must give the Spirit of God time to work. Let the Spirit direct you and not vice versa.

With that in mind, what's the procedure one ought to follow in turning a conversation to spiritual things? Notice I use the word *procedure*. One is wise to think of it as just that—a procedure to follow instead of steps to take. Procedure represents flow—a "flow" in terms of how to move the direction of a conversation to spiritual things.

"Plow and Pursue"

An overruling principle ought to preside over every conversation you have with a non-Christian. That overriding principle is—*plow and pursue.*

Plow into the conversation, enjoying it immensely. As you talk, ask questions related to three areas where non-Christians are experts. Those three areas are their family, their job, and their background. Notice I said, "Ask questions." Those who are effective in turning conversations to spiritual things do not concentrate on talking. Instead, they concentrate on listening. As they listen they pursue any way possible to turn a given conversation from the here-and-now to the hereafter.

The questions we ought to ask surrounding a non-Christian's family, job, and background are ones like:

Where are you from?
Were you born there?
How long have you lived here?
Do you enjoy where you're living now?
Are you married?
Where is your wife (or husband) from?
Do you have any brothers or sisters?
Where do they live?
How many are in your present family?
What are their interests?
What do you do for a living?
How long have you worked there?
Do you enjoy it?
What do you or don't you enjoy?
Have any hobbies?
What do you do for rest and relaxation?
If you could do anything you wanted to for a job, what would it be?

Notice two things. One is that these questions demonstrate an interest in that person as an individual. The second is that it enables me to get to know where this person is coming from. Bear in mind that this is a conversation with a live human being. It can, therefore, go in almost one hundred directions at the same time. That's why these questions do not represent any set order. There are many more like them that can be asked in any order as the conversation demands.

This type of conversation lends itself to a very casual and non-threatening approach—an approach in which the non-Christian begins to understand that I am sincerely interested in him as a person. It causes him to lower his defenses as I begin asking some personal questions and eventually begin turning the conversation to spiritual things.

The entire time I'm having this kind of free flowing conversation, I'm listening for a possible way to get into spiritual things. A comment about the outdoors may allow me to talk about how impressed I am with the Creator. Disgruntlement with his marriage might allow me to be transparent about my own marriage and how spiritual things have been the biggest source of help to my wife and I as we have learned how to adjust to each other. Unhappiness with his job might give me the opportunity to talk about unhappiness in general and lead into the discussion, "Where *do* people find happiness?" A comment about an ailing child may allow me to talk about the agonizing moments of life when people we care deeply about are ill. A simple comment like, "Those moments will really drive you to your knees in prayer," has and can open up a good discussion about spiritual things.

Suppose with all that plowing and pursuing nothing surfaces in the areas of family, job, and background that allows me to reference spiritual things. If it is an enjoyable conversation, it may be appropriate to pick up on something that person has said about life in general and ask questions similar to:

Why do you suppose the problems in the world seem to be getting worse instead of better?
What in your opinion is the number one thing most people are looking for in their lives?
Why do you think so many people seem unhappy with life in general?
What do you think is in store for the future?
A lot of people seem worried? What, in your opinion, worries people the most?

Abiding by the simple principle of plow and pursue gives your mind the freedom to think. Realizing there is no one way to turn a conversation allows your mind to begin to explore the possibilities.

Also bear in mind that as you are talking you are praying. You are asking God for the door of opportunity we referred to earlier. Since God is more concerned about the lost than we will ever be, we can pray with confidence that as we do our part, He will do His.

One might ask, "What about those who simply don't want to talk?" I assume an openness to me as an individual is an open door to the Gospel. If they are not even interested in conversation, I recognize that as a situation where God has to work before I can. Always keep in mind that although hindered from talking, you are not hindered from praying. With prayers that God might provide a door of opportunity, that person who is not receptive this week may be next week.

Proceed from the Secular to the Spiritual and Then to the Gospel

Tact and common sense are vital to evangelism. Both are inherent to the concept, "Do unto others as you would have them do unto you." Put yourself in the shoes of a non-Christian. Few of us would want someone to walk up to us and abruptly say, "Are you washed in the blood?" We might tell them what we'd like to wash them in! Nor would we want them to abruptly ask, "Are you going to heaven when you die?" Yet surprising as it is, I've personally seen that kind of abruptness and lack of tact demonstrated in evangelism.

Tact and common sense means one does not go from the secular to the Gospel, but instead from the secular to the spiritual and then to the Gospel. Having asked questions about family, job, and background that allow us to allude to spiritual things, one can now ask questions similar to:

Do you enjoy reading about religious topics or subjects?
Have you become involved in any church in your area?
Have you ever examined some of the teachings of the Bible?
With so many interests, are you interested in spiritual things?
Why do you think a lot of people across the world have interest in some kind of religion or another?
From time to time a lot of people talk about Christ and Christians. Who, in your opinion, is Jesus Christ?

It is *then* that I am able to go into the Gospel. To do so, I simply call their attention to the fact that the most important thing in life is that we know for certain where we are going when we die. I, therefore, ask the simple question, "Has anyone ever taken a Bible and shown you how you can know you're going to heaven?" Almost always they respond, "No, they haven't." I then ask, "May I?" (Should they respond, "Yes, they have," I simply ask, "What did they show you?" How they answer determines how I proceed from there.)

I then share the Bad News/Good News with them, (which I explain in the next chapter) to help them understand that eternal life is theirs as a free gift upon simple trust in Christ.

Conclusion

Neither I, nor anybody I know, would desire to give any believer the impression that turning a conversation to spiritual things is a piece of cake. But neither would we want to give anyone the impression that it is the hardest thing on earth. Relaxing, allowing the mind to think, enjoying the conversation, and bathing the opportunity in prayer as we follow the above procedure makes a tremendous difference in the comfort level of discussing spiritual things for you as well as the person you are talking with. It may make an eternal difference in their lives. Following the simple principle of plow and pursue brings freedom, not frustration, into one of the most difficult areas of evangelism—knowing how to turn a conversation to spiritual things.

QUESTIONS FOR REFLECTION

- As you think of recent opportunities you've had to evangelize, how does the fact that there is no one way to do it "free you up" in evangelism?

- What kind of commitment are you willing to make to the Lord in terms of talking to the lost so that He can use your experience to increase your skills in evangelism and specifically turning a conversation to spiritual things?

- As you reflect upon conversations you have had with the lost, can you see ways you have hurried the conversation when a bit more patience may have made it easier to turn your interaction to spiritual things? Think of one or two instances and then reflect on how you could have handled the conversation differently.

- Without looking at the lists given in the previous chapter, how many questions can you recall that can be asked related to one's family, job, and background that could help turn a conversation to spiritual things?

- How in the past have you made turning a conversation to spiritual things more difficult by not attempting to go from the secular to the spiritual and *then* to the Gospel?

Chapter Three

How to Tell the Bad News/Good News

I have little patience with evangelists who lambaste people over the head because they don't evangelize. The reason is simple. It took me only a few years in evangelism to discover that most people would *like* to lead at least one person to Christ before they die. Their problem was they just didn't know how.

Anyone consistent in evangelism has a basic method of speaking to others about the Lord. I honestly don't know how many have told me that the most helpful thing I ever did for them was to teach the Bad News/Good News approach that I developed years ago.*

When speaking with a unbeliever, I begin by asking questions to get to know the individual. My questions, as was suggested earlier, usually concern the person's background, family, and job. As we talk, I turn the conversation to spiritual things.

Then, in preparation for presenting the Gospel, I ask a question which focuses on salvation: "Has anyone ever taken a Bible and shown

---

* This Bad News/Good News approach is available in booklet presentation for non-Christians and may be ordered through EvanTell, Inc. The booklet is titled *May I Ask You a Question?*

you how you can know you're going to heaven?" The usual reply is, "No, I don't believe anyone has." I then ask, "May I?"

At this point, I need a smooth transition into my presentation, so I say, "The Bible contains both bad news and good news. The bad news is something about you. The good news is something about God. Let's talk about the bad news first."

1. You are a sinner (Rom. 3:23).

I begin by saying, "There are several things you need to understand. The first is that you are a sinner." I turn to Romans 3:23 and *have the person read it*. The verse says, "For all have sinned and fall short of the glory of God."

Using an illustration to explain that verse, I say, "When the Bible says you and I have sinned, it means we lie, we lust, we hate, we steal, we murder, etc. The word *sin* in the Bible actually means 'to miss the mark.' In other words, God is perfect and we aren't. Let me explain! Suppose you and I were each to pick up a rock. Then I said to you, 'I want you to throw that rock and hit the North Pole.' Well, you might get it farther than I, or I might get it farther than you, but neither of us would make it. Both of us would fall short. When the Bible says that all have sinned and fall short of the glory of God, it means God has set a standard that every one of us must meet. That standard is God Himself. We must be as holy as He is holy, as perfect as He is perfect. But it doesn't matter how religiously we live or how good we are, we cannot meet the standard. All of us have sinned and fall short of the glory of God."

2. The penalty for sin is death (Rom. 6:23a).

I introduce the second point of my outline by saying, "But the bad news gets even worse. The second thing you need to understand is that the penalty for sin is death." I turn to Romans 6:23 and *have the person read to the comma*. It says, "For the wages of sin is death."

Again I use an illustration. "Suppose you were to work for me for one day and I were to pay you fifty dollars. Fifty dollars would be your wages. It represents what you have earned. The Bible is saying that because you and I have sinned, we have earned death. We are going to die and be eternally separated from God."

Having presented the bad news, I now need a transition into the good news which begins the third point of my outline. So I say, "Now I think you'll agree with me, *that* is bad news." The usual reply is, "Yes, I see what you mean." Then, I explain, "But after the Bible gives the bad news, it gives the good news. What the Bible is saying is that since there is no way you could come to God, God decided to come to you."

3. Christ died for you (Rom. 5:8).

I continue by saying, "The third thing you need to understand is that Christ died for you." I turn to Romans 5:8 and *have the person read it*. It says, "But God demonstrates His own love toward us, in that while we were still sinners, Christ died for us."

I use this illustration to explain the verse: "Let's say you were in the hospital dying of cancer. I could come to you and say, 'I want to do something for you. We'll take the cancer cells from your body and put them into my body.' What would happen to me?" The usual reply is, "You would die." I say, "Right. I would die. What would happen to you?" The usual reply is, "I would live." I then say, "Right. You would live. Now tell me why." The usual reply is, "Because you took my cancer. You died for me." I then explain, "Yes! I took the thing that was causing your death, placed it upon myself, and died as your substitute. The Bible is saying that Christ came into the world, took the sin that was causing your death, placed it upon Himself, and died in your place. He was your substitute. The third day He arose as proof that sin and death had been conquered."

4. You can be saved through faith (Eph. 2:8–9).

I introduce the final point of my outline by saying, "Now, just as the bad news got even worse, the good news gets even better. The final thing you need to understand is that you can be saved through faith." I turn to Ephesians 2:8–9 and *have the person read it*. It says, "For by grace you have been saved through faith, and that not of yourselves; it is the gift of God, not of works, lest anyone should boast."

I explain, "The word *grace* means undeserved or unmerited favor. *Saved* means to be rescued or delivered from the penalty of sin. Now, you are probably wondering, 'What is faith?' The word *faith* means 'trust.'"

I again use an illustration to explain the Scripture. I say, "Since Jesus Christ has died for your sins, God can now give you heaven as a free gift. All you need to do is put your faith or your trust in Christ. For example, you were not there when that chair you are sitting in was made, and you didn't examine how it was built before you sat down. You are simply trusting the chair to hold you. Putting your faith in Christ means trusting Him to save you—not trusting your church membership, your good life, or your baptism to get you to heaven, but trusting Christ and Him alone. Your trust has to be in the One who died for you and arose. It is then that God gives you heaven as a free gift."

At this point, I use a concluding question which invites the person to trust Christ. I ask, "Is there anything that is keeping you from trusting Christ as your Savior right now?" Many times the reply is, "No, I just never understood it before." I then ask, "Would you like to pray and tell God that you are trusting His Son as your Savior?" The frequent reply is, "Yes, I would."

I then have the person tell me how I can go to heaven to make certain he understands. If he does, I do one of two things. I either lead him in prayer or have him pray. I let the person choose which he would rather do. Usually people like the idea of me praying aloud and then praying aloud with me. But before doing either, I make certain he understands that saying a prayer has never saved anyone. *Prayer is only the means by which people tell God they are trusting Jesus Christ as their Savior.* The prayer I have the person repeat after me goes something like this: "Dear God, I come to you now. I know that I am a sinner. I believe Christ died for me and arose. Right now, I trust Jesus Christ as my Savior. Thank you for the forgiveness and everlasting life I now have. In Jesus' name, Amen."

After the person trusts Christ, I want him to understand that assurance of everlasting life is based on fact, not feeling. So I turn to John 5:24 and *have the person read it.* It says, "Most assuredly, I say to you, he who hears My word and believes in Him who sent Me has everlasting life, and shall not come into judgment, but has passed from death into life."

Then I say to the person, "Now, let's go back and look at each verb in the verse. It says, 'He who *hears* My word . . .' Did you do that?" He usually replies, "Yes." I say, "'And *believes* in Him who sent Me . . .' Did you believe what God said and trust Christ as your Savior?" He says, "Yes, I did." I continue, "'*Has* everlasting life.' Does that mean later or right now?" He replies, "Right now." I read on, "'And *shall not* come into judgment.' Does that say, 'shall not' or 'might not'?" He replies, "It says, 'shall not'!" I point to the last verb and say, "'But *has passed* from death into life.' Does that say, 'has passed' or 'will pass'?" He responds, "Has passed." I conclude, "In other words, you now have everlasting life on the basis of fact, not feeling." I encourage the person to commit this verse to memory.

At this point, one of two things happens: (1) I share with him several things which will help him grow as a Christian. I emphasize prayer, Bible study (recommending he start with Philippians), baptism, and involvement in a Bible-believing church; or (2) I arrange to get together with him at another time to talk about how to grow as a Christian.

The Presentation Outlined

Introduction Question:
"Has anyone ever taken a Bible and shown you how you can know you're going to heaven? May I?"

I. Bad News
    A.   You are a sinner.
        Romans 3:23
        "Rock"
    B.   The penalty for sin is death.
        Romans 6:23
        "Wages"

II. Good News
    A.   Christ died for you.
        Romans 5:8
        "Cancer"
    B.   You can be saved through faith.
        Ephesians 2:8–9
        "Chair"

Concluding Question:
"Is there anything that is keeping you from trusting Christ as your Savior right now?"

Conclusion

Some of the most helpful advice I could give anyone who wants to be consistent in evangelism would be the three words: master a method. That way when you are face-to-face with a lost person, wanting to share Christ but frozen with fright, you can relax in one thought. That is, as the conversation is turned to spiritual things, you know *how* you are going to present the Gospel. Having confidence in a method you have mastered does more than anything to help generate the courage you need.

Although there may be many things you are uncertain of about what the non-Christian might say or ask, your boldness is increased by the fact that you know how you are going to present the Gospel to him or her. And after all, what other message is more important to share with a non-Christian than the message of the Gospel?

QUESTIONS FOR REFLECTION

- As you think of opportunities you could have to share the Gospel in the coming weeks, what are the advantages of mastering a method of presenting the Gospel?

- Can you think through the Bad News/Good News approach without looking at the chapter you've just read?

- How does using the illustration of throwing a rock and trying to hit the North Pole help people see themselves as sinners in God's eyes?

- In what specific ways does the Bad News/Good News approach help non-Christians understand the issue is trusting Christ to save them and not their good works?

- How should the fact that the Gospel is so simple, free, and easy to explain affect your motivation in evangelism?

Chapter Four

How to Reach
Your Relatives

Few things are more distressing to a Christian than the realization that, unless something happens, those who are part of their family on earth will not be part of their family in heaven. Out of concern and compassion and often discouragement and distress, individuals ask, "How do I reach my own relatives with the Gospel?"

Several things must be kept in mind.

You Don't!

That's where you start—by recognizing that you, in and of yourself, cannot bring your relatives to Christ.

Christians often take responsibility upon their shoulders in this area. Frustrations arise such as, "Why can't my family see it? Why don't they listen?"

This concern for their salvation is healthy, the inner frustration is not. If not handled properly, it can lead to feelings of guilt, and even bitterness or anger. Instead, you must recognize that unless the Spirit of God dispels the darkness from their minds and eyes and causes them to see their need, they will never come to Christ.

Second Corinthians 4:3–4 is as true for members of your family as it is for anyone else. "But even if our gospel is veiled, it is veiled to those who are perishing, whose minds the god of this age has blinded, who do not believe, lest the light of the gospel of the glory of Christ, who is the image of God, should shine on them." Your own relatives will only come to Christ the same way and time you did—when the Spirit of God dispels the darkness and causes them to see their need. Jesus said, "No one can come to Me unless the Father who sent Me draws him" (John 6:44).

That is why you must commit yourself to fervent prayer and encourage several others to join you. Whatever you do—don't get discouraged. My own parents came to a point of assuring me that their trust was in Christ alone for their salvation after twenty-seven years of prayer!

Do you lack faith that God could bring your own relatives to Christ? Many do. They can envision God saving the most renowned atheist more quickly than their own relatives.

How do you pray in faith when you lack faith? Think of those God has brought to Himself that, humanly speaking, you would have deemed harder to reach than your own relatives. You may think of a criminal, drug addict, or extremely religious individual. Then remind yourself that the God who delights in difficult and impossible situations can save your loved ones just as He has saved others. With that in mind, continue to pray in faith.

For years I was forced to take my own advice. The thing I wanted so desperately was for my mom and dad to assure me their trust was in Christ alone for their salvation—not their good works or their membership in a church. The thought *Will it ever happen?* often plagued my mind. Almost immediately I would force myself to think of "God's stories"—those people I saw Him bring to Himself in outreaches—the teenager who one week earlier had attempted suicide, the man whose mother was married so many times he could have written the book on rough childhoods, and the woman who aborted her child months earlier. I then told God, "If you could save them, you can save my folks." When exactly dad and mom crossed the line in terms of trusting Christ I'll not be sure until I see Him face-to-face. It may have been many years earlier when the denominational church they were in was preaching the Gospel. It may have been shortly before they died. Either way, dad assured me he had settled the issue and was anxious to be with the Lord. Mom went to be with the Lord echoing her conviction, "Jesus saves."

A Verbal Witness Is Not Your Only Choice

When it comes to witnessing to relatives, most people forget the post office. The post office could be an instrument used by God to assist in bringing your relatives to Christ through the simple transportation of a letter from your home to the home of a lost relative.

Letters have a tremendous advantage. Unlike a conversation that goes in one ear and out the other, your relatives will read letters—and reread them—even though they may never tell you they received them. This, though, is not a one page letter. It's closer to a ten-page one. It's one where you take time and thought to write about four things.

A Confession—Is there something wrong you have done to them that's like a clog in the pipe—something holding back the flow of communication from your heart to theirs? Perhaps you were one big headache during your teenage years. Perhaps your dishonesty on numerous occasions still haunts your witness to them. If so, get it out on the surface. A simple and sincere "I'm sorry" may do more to allow the Spirit of God to work than you've ever thought possible. There is certainly no need for confession where confession is not needed, but there is a need for confession where wrong has been done.

A Compliment—Compliment them for what they've meant to you. Even the worst relative has something you can find to compliment. Did they provide for so many of your needs? Did they send you a card on Mother's Day or Father's Day? Did they provide a warm house on a cold night? Was there an event or outing they took you on that was one of those "never to be forgotten" times? Did they assist you financially while you were in college? Were they thoughtful in remembering your birthday each year?

Your Concern—They need to know that one of your first and foremost concerns is that you want your loved ones to be with you in heaven. As I once said to my dad in a letter, "You are one of the finest fathers a son could have. I hope I can be as good a father to my son as you were to me. But what does that mean if we are not together in heaven? I want more than anything else for us to be together in heaven." Speak heart to heart and let your concern and compassion flow through your pen and onto your letter.

The Cross—Explain to them God's simple plan of salvation and, above all else, *be clear!* To come to Christ they must recognize they are sinners and no amount of goodness will get them into heaven. But Jesus Christ, God's perfect Son, died on the cross in their place and as their substitute, taking the punishment for their sins. The third day He rose victoriously. For that reason, through simple trust in Christ alone as their only way to heaven, they can receive the free gift of life eternal. Bear in mind that should God work through your letter, your loved ones will be asking themselves, "How do I settle the issue of my salvation? What do I do?" You might encourage them by saying something in your letter such as, "If you feel like you understand God's plan of salvation for the first time, just get alone with the Lord somewhere and tell Him, in your own words, that you recognize that you are a sinner, and that you now understand Christ died for you and rose again, and right now you are trusting Him to save you. Wherever you are at that moment, God will give you eternal life as a free gift."

Do you direct their attention to Scripture? By all means do. It is best to write out the verses for them instead of having them be distracted by finding a Bible (which they may not have) and attempting to look them up.

Would not an evangelistic tract enclosed in the letter accomplish the same thing? I am a firm believer in the use of evangelistic tracts and always carry one in my pocket for those God brings across my path. In this situation, however, your relatives need the plan of salvation from you and the verses you write out, not the words of another author.

Should you enclose a tract they will most likely lay it aside as they continue reading your letter. In so doing, they hear your words but not His. A letter that incorporates His words among yours is likely to prevent that from happening.

Is such a letter effective if the loved ones are across town instead of across the country? Very definitely. The location is not the issue. The fact that you took the time and had the concern to write such a lengthy letter is.

You Are Not the Only Person to Reach Them

God uses human instruments to bring people to Christ. That's why Jesus said, "The harvest truly is great, but the laborers are few;

therefore pray the Lord of the harvest to send out laborers into His harvest" (Luke 10:2). Sometimes those outside the family can be more effective in speaking to a non-Christian relative than those inside.

After leading a man to Christ, he exclaimed to me, "I'm going to call my brother. He is going to be so excited to hear that I've trusted Christ." After questioning him further about the situation, I discovered what is often the case. This man received a message from me that he stubbornly refused to accept from his own brother. One reason he found it easier to listen to me was simple: I was not a member of his family.

With that in mind, ask God to send an *additional* witness to speak to your non-Christian family member. Remember—God knows where such a person is even if you don't. A Christian you may not even know may be the one God uses to bring your family member to Christ.

As you pray for such a person, ask God to provide an opportunity (Col. 4:3) and grant boldness to the one who is sharing the Gospel (Acts 4:29).

Bear in mind I used the terms "an *additional* witness." That means, somebody in addition to you, not somebody instead of you. Continue to do what you can as God gives opportunity, while you pray for that additional witness.

Consistency Speaks Loudly

Relatives who will not listen to what you have to say may instead look at the way you live. Live the kind of consistent Christian life that attracts non-Christian family members to the Savior. Follow the kind of advice Peter gives wives with non-Christian husbands: "Be submissive to your own husbands, that even if some do not obey the word, they, without a word, may be won by the conduct of their wives" (1 Peter 3:1).

A man antagonistic for years to the Gospel finally came to Christ. He attributed his conversion to a neighbor who was very timid. When the neighbor realized the man's conversion was because of him, he expressed surprise saying, "I never spoke to you about Christ the way I should have." The new Christian responded, "No, you didn't. But you lived me to death. I could refute others' arguments and upset their logic, but I could not refute the way you lived."

Does that mean you dare never fail? Not at all. In one area or another, all Christians can and will fail. Non-Christians are not turned off by Christians who fail, they are turned off by Christians who deceive. It is one thing to fail, it is another thing to not even attempt to live for Christ, while at the same time trying to persuade someone else of their need for Him. A non-Christian once remarked, "The people I thought were Christians had lives that were singularly the same as mine. They fought with their wives, beat their kids, searched for homes in the suburbs, weren't loving, and weren't being loved. I always thought that if Christianity existed, it must exist in the lives of people. So my obvious conclusion was, it didn't exist."

A related question asked is, "What about my life before I came to Christ?" Believers often add, "My folks know all about me—my drug addiction, temper, and the many problems I caused them." Satan is a master of intimidation. He loves to say, "Don't bother speaking to others about Christ—especially your own family. Look at the rabble-rouser you used to be." Refuse to let Satan intimidate you. Honesty is the best policy. Be willing to admit to being the person you used to be, live in His forgiveness, and let others see your changed life. The issue is never where you were. The issue is, where are you *now?* Even those who wish to throw the past in your face have to recognize in their quiet, contemplative moments that God has changed your life and can certainly change theirs. If they insist on bringing up your past, a proper response would be, "I'm not in any way proud of some things I've done in the past. But that is one reason I'm so glad I came to Christ when I did. I wish somebody would have explained God's free gift to me earlier the way I hope you will understand it now."

Conclusion

The God who brought you to Christ can save any non-Christian relative. As I've told many, God has never met a person His heart did not love or His arm could not reach. The "whoever" of John 3:16 assures that—"For God so loved the world that He gave His only begotten Son, that whoever believes in Him should not perish but have everlasting life." If you do your part, God will do His. Pray—write—live—do all you can to commend the Savior to them. Sooner than you may think, as they trust the Savior they may say, "Thanks for not giving up on me," as you welcome them into the forever family.

QUESTIONS FOR REFLECTION

- How could the circumstances of your own conversion encourage you that if God could reach you He can certainly reach your relatives?

- What is the difference between asking God to send someone *instead* of you to speak to your relatives and asking God to send someone in *addition* to you?

- Who are the first relatives that come to mind that you would like to write a letter to explaining your burden for their salvation?

- How has Satan intimidated you with your past mistakes?

- As you think of your own experiences, especially before your conversion, why do you suppose consistency in a Christian's life has such an impact upon non-Christians?

Chapter Five

How to Respond
to a Cultist

You heard they were in the neighborhood. Now they are right on your doorstep.

Clearly they are on a mission. It may stem from the height of dedication or the depth of deception. They may want you to come to their place of worship or consider their publication. Some may be accommodating, others may be argumentative. But they *are* on a mission. With your involvement, they would like to increase their number by one!

Often referred to as simply "cultists," they espouse a founder, leader, and savior other than the Person of Jesus Christ and do not agree with the central teachings of Christianity. As a believer in Jesus Christ, what do you do when cultists comes calling?

To begin, let's establish two basic biblical truths.

You Are There to Talk to Them

When God brings cultists to your door or anywhere across your path, God did not bring them there for *them* to talk to *you*. He brought them there for *you* to talk to *them*. The reason is that the biblical message of salvation is very clear. You come to God as a sinner, recognize Jesus Christ died in your place as your substitute and arose, and place your trust in Christ alone to get you to heaven. Once you do, God gives you His gift of life eternal completely free. Those who have received and appropriated that message are invited to be His disciples and tell others about Him. The first thing Christ ever taught His disciples is recorded in Matthew 4:19, "Follow Me, and I will make you fishers of men."

With that in mind, God brings cultists across your path for the same reason that He brings others across your path—that you might bring them the good news of the Gospel. Since the cultists are coming with an apparent interest in spiritual things, you have the opportunity and the privilege of being the bearer of good news. God did not bring them there for them to talk to you. God brought them there for you to talk to them. They do not have a message you need to hear. Instead you have a message they need to hear.

You Must Know What You Believe

Believers have often been told, "To reach cultists you must know what they believe." Often, believers study the fine points of a doctrine taught by a particular cult and how to refute each point. This becomes a bit frustrating when one realizes how many new cults are developing each year. How does one keep up with their teachings? It is compounded by the fact that even members of established cults do not agree amongst themselves. Members of the Church of Jesus Christ of the Latter-Day Saints (Mormons) do not agree with all the teachings of the Church of Jesus Christ of Latter-Day Saints Reorganized!

Most people in a cult are not members because they have thought through the teachings of the cult and are convinced of them. They are involved because, as a national magazine once stated, someone gave them "a sense of belonging." They are members because they found a friend, not because they found the truth.

Ephesians 4:14 says to the believer that we should so grow in our knowledge of Christ "that we should no longer be children, tossed to and fro and carried about with every wind of doctrine, by the trickery of men, in the cunning craftiness by which they lie in wait to deceive." Simply put, you must know biblical truth so well that when error comes across your path you recognize it and identify it as such.

When the FBI trains its agents to recognize counterfeit money, they do so by having them study authentic bills. That way, when the counterfeit money comes across their path, they can identify it as such. To reach cultists you don't have to know what *they* believe. You must know what *you* believe. With these two basic truths in mind, let's outline four helpful principles for when a cultist comes calling.

Principle #1
Center on Two Items

Bear in mind that since God allowed the cultists to cross your path so you could explain the Gospel to them, *you* are to lead the discussion. The way to do so is to kindly but firmly request that your conversation be centered around two items. Those two items are (1) Who is Jesus Christ? and (2) Is heaven free?

Why? That is the basis of our salvation—eternal life is a free gift because Jesus Christ, God's perfect Son, died and arose—and those are the two items on which all cults disagree with Scripture. Jesus Christ, to most cults, was not the one Scriptures declare Him to be—the Savior of the world. Instead, He was at best a great teacher. In addition, all cults teach that only through good deeds and dedication to the teachings of their founder will one receive eternal life. In their teaching, eternal life is anything but a free gift.

Principle #2
Talk Over an Open Bible

Jesus Christ was the master evangelist. He knew how to bring people to Himself. In John 5:39 to His own people, the Jews, He exhorted, "You search the Scriptures, for in them you think you have eternal life; and these are they which testify of Me." He then added, "But you are not willing to come to Me that you may have life." In so doing, He was not discouraging the study of the Scriptures, but instead encouraging it. He was simply saying, "Now examine what you've been taught by what you've read—not what you've read by what you've been taught."

Simply and kindly say to the cultists, "I must insist we talk over an open Bible." You will find, as I have, that some will be cooperative out of politeness and some will be annoyed out of intimidation. Bear in mind, if they respond that the Bible contains mistakes, the burden is upon them to prove it; the burden is not upon you to prove it doesn't. In any court of law, the defendant is found innocent until proven guilty. Consistency demands that same principle be applied to the Scriptures. Since God declares His word is God-breathed (2 Tim. 3:16; 2 Peter 1:20–21), it is up to them to prove it's not. You will discover most of them have never read the Scriptures.

A friend and I once asked a Mormon, "How many times have you read the book of Mormon?" She answered, "Seven times." We then asked, "How many times have you read the Bible?" She answered, "I've never read it." We then asked her, "Why then do you say (as the Mormons do) that it is not translated correctly?" Her answer was, "Because that is what my parents told me." We then confronted her with the need to study the Scriptures for herself and come to her own conclusions. Had she said to me, "Have you ever read the Book of Mormon?" I could have sincerely said, "Yes." But instead I would have said, "Yes, but even if I hadn't, it wouldn't bother me. I am examining everything by the Bible, not the Bible by everything." Insist that all conversation be over an open Bible.

You might be tempted to think, "But I don't consider myself that knowledgeable with the Bible." Bear in mind that if nothing else, in explaining what you believe you can go through the Bad News/Good News presentation of the Gospel with them. That way you will be giving them the thing they most need to hear—God's simple plan of salvation.

With that in mind, some ask, "Does not 2 John 10–11 forbid me from allowing a cultist into my house even to discuss the Scripture with him?" There we are told, "If anyone comes to you and does not bring this doctrine, do not receive him into your house nor greet him; for he who greets him shares in his evil deeds." In the New Testament context, there were no motels or hotels. Traveling speakers were dependent on others for both lodging and hospitality. To have such a person in your home would therefore be to encourage him in his words and work. The context today when one allows a cultist into his living room to talk is not the same. I offer no hospitality in terms of meals, etc. and provide no lodging. If you do what you should do in terms of your witness to him, you will be a proper instrument of discouragement, not encouragement. Therefore, it is my opinion that those verses would not forbid one from talking to a cultist in your home. But do so on the basis of an open Bible.

Principle #3
Demand Equal Time

Cultists love to monopolize time. They delight in taking thirty minutes and giving you five.

When responding to any lost person we must, as Christ was, be "full of grace and truth" (John 1:14). We dare not have truth with no grace, but neither dare we have grace with no truth. For that reason, since cultists love to monopolize time, a ground rule must be established—that of equal time. You must directly and kindly insist that if they take fifteen minutes they give you the same. I never hesitate to look at my watch as they begin talking and as they finish their presentation. Once I start, should they interrupt I remind them of our agreement.

Principle #4
Truth—Not Emotionalism—Must Be Your Authority

Some cultists love to kill you with kindness; others would simply love to kill you! I've had them put their arms around me attempting to call me their brother and I've had others become intensely angry with me. My concern, though, is never their response to me. It is always my response to them.

When Paul wrote 2 Timothy, he was writing a pastoral epistle. A pastor meets those who are believers and those who are unbelievers. Either way he insists, "And a servant of the Lord must not quarrel but be gentle to all, able to teach, patient, in humility correcting those who are in opposition, if God perhaps will grant them repentance, so that they may know the truth" (2 Tim. 2:24–25).

Should a cultist become emotional with you and you become emotional with him, one person wins—Satan. Should he become emotional with you, remain cool, calm, collected, and simply say, "The Bible says . . ." Truth becomes your authority.

A cultist I had the privilege of leading to Christ once said to me, "You explained what you believed and why you believed it without getting heated about it. I could never understand why those who have been trying to get me into their cult became so upset when I appeared to disagree." Let truth, not emotion, be your authority.

Conclusion

Cultists can be won to Christ. When they are, they are brought to Christ the same way everyone else is, such as the relatives mentioned in the previous chapter. Jesus declared, "No one can come to Me unless the Father who sent Me draws him" (John 6:44). Only Christ can dispel the blindness and cause them to see their need of a Savior. Do what is the most important thing of all—pray fervently and faithfully for them. Following these basic principles gives God something to use in bringing them to Himself. Soon they may see their sinful and rebellious condition before God and their need of a Savior. Their testimony may become like that of another convert who said, "I always thought the problem was my head. I discovered it was my heart."

QUESTIONS FOR REFLECTION

- How has the false idea that you have to know what cultists believe kept you from being bold in evangelizing them?

- Of the cults you are acquainted with, how do they err on the two questions: Who is Christ, and is heaven free?

- Why is it important to be loving but also firm when speaking to a cultist?

- What thoughts can you entertain when speaking to cultists that will keep you from becoming angry with their attitude, ideas, or false teaching and instead respond with the love of Christ?

- In the past, how do you see you have taken the defensive instead of the offensive when speaking to a member of a cult?

Chapter Six

How to Help Children
Understand the Good News

ↄ⌒ℐ⌒ↄ

Reaching children is a tremendous opportunity. If children come to Christ, they have an entire life to live for the Savior. Evangelist D. L. Moody was one time asked about the number of people who came to Christ through an outreach he had just concluded. When he gave the number, he attached the one-half to it. The individual responded, "I suppose that half was a child and the rest were adults." D. L. Moody's response was, "No, the half was an adult and the rest were children. The adult has half of his life to live for Christ. The child has his whole life."

At the same time it is a dangerous opportunity. Why? Because if one is not careful, one can so easily lead children into a false profession. A child will do almost anything you want him to do (until he becomes a teenager!), such as mouth any prayer you want him to pray, but not have the slightest idea what he is doing.

How then does one help a child clearly understand the Gospel and trust Christ? Several things will help bring a child, as the Holy Spirit works, to a point where the child knows the Lord and not simply the language.

Make the Gospel Clear

Nothing is more important in reaching children than making the Gospel clear. That means *you* have to be certain you have a clear understanding of the Gospel yourself. To come to Christ we must see ourselves as sinners, recognize that Jesus Christ, God's perfect Son, died as our substitute and rose again the third day, and trust in Christ alone as our only way to heaven.

The one book of the Bible that was specifically written to tell us how to come to Christ was the Gospel of John. John 20:31 tells us, "These are written that you may believe that Jesus is the Christ, the Son of God, and that believing you may have life in His Name." Ninety-eight times John says "believe." That means in recognizing that Jesus Christ died on a cross in our place and rose again, one must trust in Christ alone to get to heaven. I am careful to stay away from terms and phrases such as "invite Christ into your heart," "give your life to God," and "give your heart to Jesus," first and foremost because they are not the terms used in Scripture. Secondly, they do not clearly present what the Bible means by believe. If one is not careful, one can give a child the misunderstanding that a person is saved by repeating a prayer instead of trusting a Person.

We dare not speak in a confusing manner where God speaks clearly. Since the Gospel is simply that Christ died for our sins and arose (1 Cor. 15:3–4) and one is saved by believing—trusting in Christ alone to save us—that message must be made clear. It is at this point that two illustrations become helpful to explain substitution and trust.

I illustrate substitution by using the example of spanking—something every child I've ever met understands! Explain to them that if they were about to be spanked for disobedience to their mother or dad, and you took their spanking, you would be their substitute. Similarly, Jesus Christ is our substitute. He took our place on a cross, suffered the punishment for our sins, and rose again on the third day, proving He had conquered sin and the grave. That kind of illustration drives the truth of substitution home.

I illustrate trust with a chair, as I do in the Bad News/Good News approach. When I sit down in a chair, I am trusting the chair to save me from falling—nothing or nobody else. I even show children what I mean by sitting on a chair and taking my feet off the floor. I then explain we must trust Christ alone to get us to heaven—not our Sunday school attendance, or mommy or daddy—but Christ alone to save us.

Lead Them—Don't Drive Them

Children progress at different rates. Some understand the Gospel when they are five or six, some when they are seven, eight, or older. Their mental capacities are all different because the God that carved them produced them from His fingertips, not with the use of a Xerox machine. For that reason, one cannot approach a child thinking, "If Johnny understood it when he was six, Jimmy can too." Not necessarily. It is important to lead them to Christ, not drive them. Once children begin showing interest, keep reviewing and explaining the Gospel until you, through sensitivity bestowed by the Holy Spirit, sense they now understand and are ready to settle the issue—that is, trust Christ.

Our son is very intelligent. I delight in saying that because no one can accuse me of bragging. David is our adopted boy. In fact, some "dear" friends of ours once said to us, "Your son is so intelligent, you can tell he is adopted." Because he has an inquisitive mind, he probably was two years old when he first said he wanted to become a Christian. My wife, Tammy, and I sensed, however, that he didn't understand. One night when David was five and I was putting him to bed he said to me, "I want to become a Christian, but you and mom don't think I'm ready." So I said to him, "Well, we've been concerned that you understand. For example, what is sin?" He answered, "Well, sin is when you do wrong. Like if you and mommy tell me to do something and I don't do it, that's sin. God has given us His commandments and we have broken them." I then asked, "But what does the Bible mean when it says that Jesus died for you?" He answered, "Well, it's like this. Suppose I deserved a spanking and you took my spanking for me—you'd be my substitute. Christ is our substitute. He took our punishment." I then continued, "But what does believe mean?" He answered, "It means to trust. Like right now I'm sitting on the bed and trusting it to hold me. You have to trust Christ to get you to heaven, not your mommy or your daddy."

Convinced he understood (and was probably trying out for my job as an evangelist), I said, "Well, it seems like you understand. Would you like to settle it tonight?" He almost jumped out of bed as he exclaimed, "You mean tonight I *can* become a Christian?" He was just as excited the next morning as he explained to his mom what he had done. There are many things we have done wrong in raising David, but I'm grateful to God for one thing we did right—leading him, not driving him, to Christ.

Emphasize a Fact, Not a Date

As children mature, they understand God's plan of salvation better. The depth of what God went through to save us becomes more real to them. Then they wonder, "Did I really understand it when I was so young?"

Parents often do tremendous harm by saying, "Of course. You remember when you were five and you trusted Christ." The fact is, *you* undoubtedly remember it a lot better than they do. Furthermore, what if what you *think* happened didn't happen? You have now given them false assurance of their salvation.

When Scripture gives assurance of salvation, it does not go back to a date, it goes back to a fact. John 3:16 does not say, "For God so loved the world that He gave His only begotten Son, that whoever believes in Him *and knows the date* should not perish but have everlasting life." Instead it says, "Whoever believes in Him should not perish." The issue is, who are you trusting in right now to get you to heaven? If you are trusting Christ to get you to heaven, regardless of when you crossed the line, you are forever His.

Just because one person knows the date and the other one doesn't, does not change the fact that they are both saved. If a child later struggles with when she came to Christ, it is helpful to say something such as, "Mother and I think you understood it when you were seven. If you remember . . . [relate to her the circumstances], but really that doesn't matter. If you are trusting Christ to save you, you are saved, regardless of when you crossed the line." That way, whenever she has doubts she'll do what Scripture says—go back to fact, not a date.

Don't Condition Their Salvation on Their Behavior

Often, after children have come to Christ and they misbehave, we admonish them by saying, "Now do you think if you were a Christian you'd do something like that?" The biblical answer to that question is, yes. Although when people come to Christ they ought to live the holiest life they can for the Savior, Christians in the New Testament were often a far cry from what they should have been. Christians in the church in Corinth were guilty of immorality (1 Cor. 5), going to court against each other (1 Cor. 6:1–8), having a divisive spirit (1 Cor. 11:17–18), and participating in the Lord's table in a dishonoring way (1 Cor. 11:27–34). How would you like it if, when quarreling with your wife or husband, your child were to say to you, "Do you think if you were a Christian you'd argue like that?"

Don't condition their salvation on their behavior. At best, they are like you—a saved sinner. There will be times when they fail and need instruction on how to live the holiest life they can for the Savior. But that is a matter of growth. Don't make it a matter of salvation.

Conclusion

Children are dangerous opportunities. Remembering the above principles can help a child clearly understand the Gospel of grace. Make the Gospel clear. Lead them—don't drive them. Emphasize a fact, not a date. Don't condition their salvation on their behavior.

Before long you may discover something exciting. You have not only reached a child, you have reached part of another generation. The children you clearly explain salvation to will become adults with their own children. They will clearly explain salvation to their children the same way you did to them years earlier. To your gratification and eternal reward, you will have reached part of another generation for the Savior.

QUESTIONS FOR REFLECTION

- How is presenting the Gospel to a child no different than presenting it to anyone? In what ways is it different?

- Why is it easy to rush children into understanding the Gospel instead of being certain they understand the meaning of Christ's death and resurrection?

- If you presented the Gospel to a child and now wish you had made it clearer, what might you do to make sure the child understands?

- Why should all of us be grateful that our assurance of eternal life is based on a fact not a date?

- In what specific ways can we be grateful to God that He does not condition our salvation on our behavior and how should that affect our thinking about our own children?

Chapter Seven

How to Overcome
Fear in Evangelism

If most of us were honest, we'd admit we enjoy evangelism the most when:

- The person we plan to talk to is not at home.
- God allows us to do the praying and someone else to do the talking.
- The individual we are approaching has laryngitis and therefore it would be impolite to ask him about his relationship with Christ.
- The waitress explains to our friend that she has a phone call just as we were preparing to approach spiritual things with her.
- We absolutely unintentionally oversleep the morning of our breakfast appointment with a non-Christian.
- As soon as we approach spiritual things with an individual, he tells us he's a Christian and we of course don't want to insult him by telling him what he probably already knows.

The reason can be reduced to one word—fear. Absolutely paralyzing at times, fear does more to hinder our witness than any other single item.

How does one overcome such a devastating problem? Can it actually be overcome? Does a person ever get to the point when fear in evangelism is a thing of the past?

All of these questions are answered for us in the Bible. Before looking for the answers, however, two things must be kept in mind.

First, fear in evangelism is normal. It assures you that you are a normal human being. After all, Paul the apostle was afraid to evangelize. How does he admit to entering Corinth? He determined to be true to the message of Christ and the cross, but he admits to being with them "in weakness, in fear, and in much trembling" (1 Cor. 2:3). In a city filled with such godlessness, impurity, and vice, such fear is certainly understandable.

Paul is not alone. Peter and John had equal reason to be afraid. In Acts 4, we have the first recorded persecution experienced by the early church. Commanded not to speak or teach in the name of Jesus (v. 18), what do Peter and John do—hover in a corner, pray for the rapture, or plead with God to "send Joe"? Not for a minute! Instead, we are taught that they laid their fears before God. "Now, Lord, look on their threats, and grant to Your servants that with all boldness they may speak Your word" (Acts 4:29).

If people with that kind of commitment to the Savior are afraid, why would we not be? After all, fear in evangelism has nothing to do with the presence or lack of spirituality. It has everything to do with being human. We dare not assume that because we are afraid, there is something wrong with our walk with the Lord. How we deal with our fear may be *affected* by our walk with the Lord, but the *presence* of fear itself is never attributed in Scripture to a lack of spiritual depth.

With that in mind, a second thing to remember is that the issue is *overcoming* fear, not removing fear. I am absolutely convinced that this side of heaven one will always have times of fear. Paul the apostle requested prayer that "utterance may be given to me, that I may open my mouth boldly to make known the mystery of the gospel" (Eph. 6:19). When Paul wrote these words he was writing them as a prisoner in Rome. When he was in prison he had time to think back on his evangelistic experiences. Paul had spent three years in Ephesus and God used him mightily. Not only had he established a strong Christian church in Ephesus, he also sent out messengers through whom the whole province of Asia was evangelized. Churches were established in each of its major population centers.

You mean Paul the apostle is actually requesting prayer for boldness in evangelism after his extensive experience? Most certainly. He knew full well that once fear raises its ugly head and is dealt with, it is not gone forever—never having to be dealt with again. Instead of thinking in terms of never being afraid, Paul had to think in terms of overcoming fear each time it became a major obstacle to sharing the Gospel.

Moments of fear will always be there. Anyone who says they are never afraid to share Christ is most likely not being honest with you. Evangelists have often admitted to their own fear in speaking the Savior's name to others. I have discovered it is less threatening to present Christ from the pulpit than it is one-on-one. Audiences don't tend to answer back like individuals do. One simply has to learn what to do each time fear arises so that it may be overcome. Through responding properly, on a consistent basis, boldness has the upper hand over fear. Those who share Christ constantly do not do so because they are never afraid. They do so because each time boldness takes over fear instead of fear taking over boldness.

With that in mind, how do we as normal human beings and believers in Christ experience the boldness that overcomes fear?

Nowhere is there a verse in the Bible that says, "Now here is how you overcome fear." But when one takes the Scriptures and examines them carefully, one can learn much from the examples of others. At least five things will help us experience the victory any believer committed to evangelism desires in this area.

Talk to God About Your Fear

How many times have you heard believers confess to one another, "My biggest problem in evangelism is fear. I am so afraid of being rejected"? The problem is that they often tell scores of believers their fear but too rarely confess it to Christ. The difference should be obvious. As helpful as telling others may be, there is no one on earth who can lend the aid He can. He ought to be the first we express the difficulty to, not the last.

As we do so, what we are specifically asking God for is courage or boldness. The courage that makes us go ahead *despite* our fears. The courage that makes us speak up, not clam up. The courage that produces the "I want to" evangelize not just the "I should."

After all, as we observed, that *is* what the apostles did in Acts 4. That *is* what Paul does in Ephesians 6. In fact, what is striking about the Ephesians 6 passage is that when Paul discusses his fear in evangelism, he does it not to complain or make excuses but simply to ask them to pray for him. We must first and foremost talk to God about our fears, not just to people.

As we do so, we must pray in faith. Nowhere in Scripture does God promise to answer prayer. He only promises to answer the prayer of faith. As we ask God in faith to give boldness we can do so with excitement and expectation because *the* Person we are talking to is the One "who is able to do exceedingly abundantly above all that we ask or think" (Eph. 3:20). I can testify firsthand that I have never once asked God for boldness that He did not provide.

Focus on What God Thinks of People, Not on What People Think of You

Fear in evangelism often results in being too self-focused. Notice that I used the word *self-focused,* not *selfish.* Most people I've observed who want to talk to acquaintances about Christ are not selfish people. The very fact that they are concerned about somebody else's eternal welfare and not just their own says so. Selfish people are content to go to heaven alone. Selfless people are not.

Self-focus is different. It results from worrying too much about what others might think of you if you share the Gospel with them. Questions such as, "Will they still be my friend?" "Will they think less of me?" "Will I lose respect?" hinder evangelism. Nobody in their right mind would enjoy any of these negative responses. Who wants to lose a friend, be thought less of, or lose respect? At the same time, "I" is at the center of all of these worries. Focusing on yourself becomes distracting at its least, defeating at its worst.

There are two words consistently used in Scripture that help refocus our attention. The first word is *love.* Biblically defined, it means to put the other person first, even if it means the sacrifice of ourselves. John 3:16 explains, "For God so loved the world that He gave His only begotten Son, that whoever believes in Him should not perish but have everlasting life." The proof of God's love is that He put us first even though it meant the sacrifice of His own Son. The second is the word *compassion*. It means to be filled with pity. Matthew 9:36 tells us, "But when He saw the multitudes, He was moved with compassion for them, because they were weary and scattered, like sheep having no shepherd." Jesus Christ pitied non-Christians.

Both of these words switch the focus to how Christ feels about the lost, not how they feel about us. Furthermore, if Jesus Christ was willing to sacrifice His *life* for us, we ought to be willing to sacrifice friendship, pride, or respect. In fact, it is only a matter of time before Chirstlike love and compassion overcome fear. Possible rejection takes a back seat to the real issue of salvation. Knowing that we have a message that will save them from eternal separation from God and give them life that has meaning, purpose, and fulfillment becomes the focus.

To be consistently bold in evangelism, we must focus on what God thinks of them, not what they think of us.

Concentrate on the Beauty of the Message and the Privilege of Being Its Messenger

After what happened in Philippi, Paul easily could have entered Thessalonica with the attitude, "I'm sick of this evangelism stuff. It is the best way I've ever heard of to win enemies and drive away friends. And besides, I've never hurt so bad. Why should I invite physical abuse?" Since many felt that Paul and Silas' preaching was aimed at the idol worship of Rome, a charge of treason resulted. Although Paul and Silas' execution was imminent, the people pounced upon them, and within moments, had them half naked, whipped, and sitting with their feet suspended in stocks. Yet Paul was able to testify, "But even after we had suffered before and were spitefully treated at Philippi, as you know, we were bold in our God to speak to you the gospel of God in much conflict" (1 Thess. 2:2). Unlike other speakers whose messages were full of deceit, uncleanness, and guile (1 Thess. 2:3), Paul recognized he had only truth and good news, not error and bad news to give them.

When a person is so gripped by a message another needs to hear, everything else becomes insignificant in comparison. The one bearing the message has the attitude, "If you miss this, you have missed everything." So "lost" do they become in their message, that the results of speaking it are immaterial. The urge that compels them is like that of the apostles who said, "We cannot but speak the things which we have seen and heard" (Acts 4:20).

It was an overwhelming thing to Paul that God entrusted him with such a significant and life-changing eternal message: "But as we have been approved by God to be entrusted with the gospel, even so we speak, not as pleasing men, but God who tests our hearts" (1 Thess. 2:4). That privilege was not taken lightly. He knew that the One who entrusted him with that message would continue to examine his heart. So he spoke as a person with an extremely high calling—the awesome privilege of bearing the good news of the Gospel to somebody else. Simply put, his focus was on what came from his own lips, not any kind of ridicule that could come from theirs.

The beauty of that message and the privilege of being its messenger needs to grip us as well. When it does, it becomes something everyone needs to hear and our preference is that they hear it from us.

Nobody Overcomes Fear Without Evangelizing

"Dream on" as one might, fear in evangelism is never conquered in a classroom. It is only studied in a classroom. To overcome fear, two items are absolutely essential: obedience and experience.

Obedience is first, because common sense tells us without obedience there never is experience. It is simple obedience to a given command that leads to life experience.

Believers are individuals who have trusted Jesus Christ as their only way to heaven. Disciples are those who follow after Him and keep learning from Him. The first thing Jesus taught His disciples was evangelism. "Follow me, and I will make you fishers of men" (Matt. 4:19). This was accomplished by teaching them obedience. After a fruitless night of fishing, Jesus commanded them to throw out the nets once more. They did, and caught a miraculous number of fish. It was after this illustration that He told them to become fishers of men. Like Peter, we must be willing to say, "at Your word I will let down the net" (Luke 5:5).

Another example of obedience is recorded in Acts chapter 4. The Sanhedrin threatened Peter and John and commanded them not to speak nor teach in the name of Jesus. The response of Peter and John was immediate. There was no, "Would you allow us a day or two to pray about it?" or "Your Highness, we will give what you are saying careful consideration." Instead it was, "Whether it is right in the sight of God to listen to you more than to God, you judge" (v. 19). While the Sanhedrin was questioning the audacity of those who would so boldly mention the news of Christ, the apostles were questioning the audacity of those who would judge their orders to be above the Almighty's. It is quite plain they felt they were under marching orders to which disobedience was not an option.

Again, in Acts chapter 5, the apostles were brought before the Sanhedrin because they did not obey the command to stop preaching the name of Jesus. The high priest's complaint against the apostles is clear. "Did we not strictly command you not to teach in this name? And look, you have filled Jerusalem with your doctrine, and intend to bring this Man's blood on us!" (5:28). That has to be the ultimate guilt trip. Their complaint was, "You blew it on two counts. You did something you were not supposed to do and you are going to get us in trouble by your doing it." The leadership was afraid that the people stirred up by the apostles' teaching might take them to task for having condemned Jesus. Once more, though, Peter's response was immediate, "We ought to obey God rather than men" (v. 29).

God honors obedience. The humble, dependent heart that says, "I'm scared—terrified would be a better word—and don't even feel like I know how to evangelize, but you're the Master. I'm the disciple. I'll do it." God then honors obedience and answers the cry of a contrite heart. I've never met a single person who overcame fear apart from simple obedience to a God-given command.

With that obedience comes much needed experience—the experience that plays a big part in overcoming fear. Believers are so often intimidated in evangelism by what they *think* will happen or what *might* happen, instead of what does happen. Experience teaches us how to prepare for reality, knowing full well what reality is—some could care less about the Savior and His message and some could not care more. Those who could not care more become so exciting to reach that one simply tolerates the closed doors en route to the open ones.

Experience brings skills in evangelism such as how to turn a conversation to spiritual things, how to answer questions and objections, and how to clearly and concisely present the Gospel—all of which are often elements of our fear. For some, these elements are more intimidating than the fear of rejection. More than once a person has said to me, "I don't mind being rejected. I can handle that. I just don't know how to answer when someone says . . ." To counter these fears, we need good solid training in evangelism— something few believers have had. But we also need experience for which there is no substitute. There are lessons in evangelism that can only be learned through face-to-face, eyeball to eyeball contact with the lost.

When these two are combined—obedience and experience—they play an immense role in overcoming fear. God honors obedience, and experience teaches us how to respond to and overcome the obstacles that intimidate us. It is therefore no wonder that those who consistently evangelize, although experiencing struggles in the area of fear, have also experienced the most victory. God is working as they are working. Obedience and experience cause boldness to take the upper hand.

Growing Christians Have Reason to Be Bolder Than Non-Growing Ones

As we study the Scriptures, one learns very quickly that we cannot separate spiritual growth from evangelism. The closer we get to the heart of Christ, the closer we get to the people for whom He died. His heart bleeds for the *lost*. Mark 10:45 tells us, "For even the Son of Man did not come to be served, but to serve, and to give His life a ransom for many." Luke 19:10 explains, "For the Son of Man has come to seek and to save that which was lost."

My son loves Star Trek. As far as I know, there is not one episode he has not seen. He is a Star Trek freak! To be close to him is to capture his heart for Star Trek—its prominent stars and stories. Those who live close to Christ capture His heart for the lost. They bleed for the same people He bleeds for. In some way or another, whether by helping with an evangelistic outreach through the church, witnessing to a lost person, or working for an evangelistic association, they want to be used by God to populate heaven.

Christian growth and consistent living is attained by studying the Word. As 2 Timothy 3:16 tells us, "All Scripture is given by inspiration of God, and is profitable for doctrine, for reproof, for correction, for instruction in righteousness." That means every time we study the Bible, God wants to take out of our lives what should not be there and put in what should be there. This is exactly what God does when Christians study the Word. This enables them to live consistent Christian lives. Does that mean they never fail? Not for a moment. Despite mistakes and failures in Christian living, any who know them well will testify to the fact that they are growing believers—ones who are consistently learning more about the Savior and applying it to their lives.

How does that affect boldness in evangelism? For the very practical reason that growing believers do not have to consider witnessing to a lost person thinking, "I sure hope he doesn't find out how I live and how I treat my family. I have to be sure he doesn't find out how dishonest I am in business." Instead, they can walk up to a lost person knowing that they are attempting to live a consistent Christian life.

Paul the apostle verifies how such consistency provides boldness. In 1 Thessalonians 2, as he talks about his witness among the Thessalonians, he says, "You are witnesses, and God also, how devoutly and justly and blamelessly we behaved ourselves among you who believe" (v. 10). Paul's life was such a contrast to the lives of those around him, he could boldly talk of his relationship to the Savior.

Suppose that had not been Paul's character and conduct. How could he have faced a Thessalonian society with courage telling them of a Savior who could pardon their sins and save them from eternal punishment? The understandable "pressure" one feels by living a deceitful, dishonest, two-tongued, and two-sided life melts away courage.

That does not mean God cannot use a hypocrite to lead people to Christ. More than once a church leader has led people to Christ while living a sinful life in secret. There are two ways God can work—*through us* or *in spite of us*. When He uses such people He is working in spite of them more than through them. As a speaker once said, "God sometimes uses a crooked arrow to hit His mark." They probably would admit though that they do not experience the consistent courage that one who is walking in step with the Savior experiences.

Boldness in evangelism is parallel to our growth as a Christian. As our walk with Christ increases, so does our boldness. When one is in love with the Savior, one's foremost desire is to honor Him. What others think of us matters little. Our desire to honor God could not matter more.

Conclusion

Fear in evangelism is normal and natural. This side of heaven it will occur and reoccur. To say, "I don't witness because I'm afraid" is an explanation. It dare not become an excuse. The issue is what we do with our fear. With the above cautions and Scriptural principles in mind, we can come to a point of evangelizing consistently and courageously. On a regular basis, we will echo what the disciples said, "We ought to obey God rather than men." When we stand before the King of Kings to be rewarded for our faithfulness in evangelism, we will have the tremendous satisfaction of knowing our faithfulness did not result from the lack of fear but that by His grace we overcame the fear.

QUESTIONS FOR REFLECTION

- Why do you think we often confess our fears in evangelism to one another but all too rarely confess them to the Lord?

- If God were writing a paragraph to describe a non-Christian friend of yours, what do you think He would write?

- How does "getting lost in the message" often affect the way believers talk to others about Christ?

- As you think of believers you know who are bold in evangelism, can you see how their obedience expressed through experience has increased their boldness?

- How have the times when you've been closest to the Lord affected your concern for lost people?

Chapter Eight

How to Evangelize
Out of Grace, Not Guilt

∫

"If there was one word I wish were not in the Christian vocabulary, it is the word *evangelism*." I've heard that comment several times from believers. The attitude behind it is one reason why such a small percentage of believers (some estimates are five percent) ever lead someone to Jesus Christ.

The situation is compounded by the fact that even when Christians do evangelize, we often do it out of guilt—feeling that we *have* to, not that we *want* to. One believer candidly asked me, "Do you ever get to the point that you do it out of grace, not out of guilt?"

The solution is to address evangelism from a biblical perspective. When we look at evangelism from the proper perspective, the question is not, "Why does God tell me to evangelize?" but, "Why does He *allow* me to?" Four observations will help us develop this attitude.

Evangelism Is Always Approached in Scripture As a Privilege, Not As a Pain

What was the first thing Christ taught His disciples? It was not how to manage money or raise a Christian family, as important as those are. It was something bigger. Jesus said, "Follow Me, and I will make you fishers of men" (Matt. 4:19).

A fisher of fish takes something alive and makes it dead. A fisher of men takes something dead and makes it alive. Jesus was in essence saying, "With Me, your life can have eternal perspective. It will count for something that will last forever." Furthermore, "I will make you" implies, "I'll teach you everything you need to know. Just follow. I'll do the teaching if you'll do the learning."

"Wait a minute," someone might say. "I grew up in a church where evangelism was a means of determining if you were a Christian. You had to evangelize or you weren't saved."

Another might say, "I was made to feel that I had to present the Gospel to everyone I met. One man I knew pigeonholed people and immediately confronted them with the Gospel. I just can't do that."

In such cases, I express sympathy that they were exposed to such thinking and teaching. But I emphasize that at best those examples are explanations, not excuses. We do not have to live by the impressions we receive from others, especially if those impressions are unbiblical. God tells us to follow Scripture as our guide and gives us freedom to be ourselves.

A scriptural perspective on evangelism will help us develop healthier attitudes toward it. We can learn to profit from the good in our past experiences (such as recognizing a person's concern for the lost), while freeing ourselves from mistaken assumptions. One person told me, "The more I study Scripture, the more I see where I have brought baggage into evangelism that isn't biblical. Seeing evangelism from a biblical perspective has really set me free."

I have a friend who is an insurance agent. He says, "Selling insurance is how I provide for my family financially. What I love to do is introduce people to Jesus Christ." I have never heard my friend describe witnessing as something he *had* to do. Instead, what he can't seem to fathom is that God would allow him to have a job where he comes into contact with so many lost people. Imagine that—a businessman who is making an eternal difference in people's lives.

God is in the business of populating heaven. If you're interested, He will let you in on the privilege of assisting Him. Then the fruit of your life will last into eternity.

God Never Asks Anyone to Bring the Lost to Christ—He Only Asks Us to Bring Christ to the Lost

By nature, we take things on our shoulders God never intended us to carry. That's one reason we approach evangelism with so much anxiety and guilt. We take God's responsibility on our shoulders and then wonder what went wrong if the person does not respond to the claims of Christ.

I keep reminding people of Jesus' words, "No one can come to Me unless the Father who sent Me draws him" (John 6:44). I can't bring people to Christ. Only God can do that. I can only bring Christ to people. That's what makes evangelism so exhilarating. With each individual, I try to see where I fit into God's plan for bringing that person to Christ. I might be the tenth of fifteen people He will use, or the fourteen of twenty-six. A taste of heaven is when I'm the twenty-first of twenty-one!

While flying back to Dallas from a speaking engagement in Philadelphia several years ago, I began speaking with the man next to me. As I turned the conversation to spiritual things, I could tell God had been working in his life. The longer we talked, the more I sensed I might be the last person in the line of leading him to the Savior. "Has anybody ever taken a Bible and shown you how you can know you are going to heaven?" I asked. "No," he answered. "May I?" I responded. There, at thirty thousand feet above sea level, I had the privilege of introducing him to Christ.

Three weeks later I received a note from the man's girlfriend. "With your help and love, you have helped to answer a prayer of mine," she wrote. "I would, on the occasions that he seemed particularly receptive to the Word of God, tell him the new things I had learned and experienced . . . Now when I think of his newfound joy, I feel so much love and peace for life, God, you, and him, that I feel I will be happy forever."

I was overjoyed with the man's response that day. But even if he had not trusted Christ, I would have had the comfort of knowing I did my part. How can I be sure of that? Because months later on another plane flight I met a man who was just as open to the Gospel. After I tried every way I could think of to help him see the need of trusting Christ *now*, he said, "I just need time to think about it." I could tell that was *exactly* what he needed—just a little more time because the freeness of God's grace was so new to him. I stepped off the plane knowing I had done my part. It would now be up to someone else to pick up where I left off.

God will never ask us how many people we led to Christ. Stop counting and concentrate on conversing! God knows that apart from Him we will never lead anyone to Christ. He simply asks us to take Christ to them. As we do, sooner or later we will have the life-transforming opportunity of leading someone to the Savior.

God Is Not Asking You to Push Through Closed Doors—Simply Walk Through Open Ones

One thing that worsens our guilt-driven approach to evangelism is the mentality that we must present the Gospel to every person we meet. They *will* be receptive; otherwise, we have failed.

The fact is, I do run into closed doors. That doesn't discourage me. I simply keep looking for the open doors. It is not the four-letter word *push* that opens doors, but the six-letter word *prayer*. The apostle Paul asked the Colossian believers to pray that God "would open to us a door for the word" (Col. 4:3). While in prison and upon his release from prison, Paul invited people to pray that God would give him and his co-workers doors of opportunity for the Gospel.

How do we know who is open and who's not? If someone is open to me as a person, I assume that to be an open door for the Gospel. I go as far as I can through that door. If nothing else, I can usually give a tract or booklet for the person to read later.

We have lived in our present neighborhood for many years. Though we've been privileged to lead others to Christ, our next-door neighbors have been a closed door. Only once did that door begin to crack. As I prepared for an outreach to Russia, the man said, "I will mow your lawn for you under one condition: You show me your pictures when you return."

I was so pleased, it took me one-and-a-half seconds to respond, "It's a deal."

When I showed the pictures of Russia to the man and his wife, I was also able to explain what we did spiritually on the trip. Later I found out why the door had been closed before. The wife belongs to a prominent cult. Even today, the door is not open, but knowing how God works, it could open next week. Until then I can only pray, not push—nor live in guilt.

The Presence of Fear Does Not Mean the Absence of Love

It's been said there are two great hindrances to evangelism—a cold heart and cold feet. The problem is that we see one as the symptom of the other. We assume cold feet are proof of a cold heart.

The apostle Paul's entire ministry was driven by love. He testifies, "For the love of Christ compels us" (2 Cor. 5:14). Knowing the abundant love of Christ, Paul felt compelled to make a priority in his life what is a priority with God—the people for whom He died. Paul's heart was obviously attuned with the Savior's. So deeply concerned was he for the salvation of his own people that he testified, "My heart's desire and prayer to God for Israel is that they may be saved" (Rom. 10:1). He even stated one chapter earlier that he could wish himself separated from God if it would secure the salvation of his people. He explains, "For I could wish that I myself were accursed from Christ for my brethren, my countrymen according to the flesh" (Rom. 9:3). Paul was so captivated by the love of Christ that His love radiated through him to others.

Nevertheless, that never prevented him from having moments of fear. He still sensed the need to pray for boldness. He requested prayer that "utterance may be given to me, that I may open my mouth boldly to make known the mystery of the gospel" (Eph. 6:19).

Nowhere does Scripture state or even imply that the presence of fear means the absence of love. If someone asked me, "When was your last moment you sensed fear in evangelism?" I would tell you about the last person I witnessed to. The presence of fear, however, often says more about how much we are moved by His love than how much we aren't. Torn by fear, yet knowing the person must meet the Savior, we do what we can to make the Gospel clear. Fear is an excellent reason to fall to our knees in prayer—not a reason to jump into a pool of guilt.

For twenty-seven years I prayed for my parents' salvation, as I noted earlier, concerned with whether or not they understood eternal life was a free gift. To say I was fearful when witnessing to them was an understatement. Their attitude seemed to be, "We raised a preacher, didn't we? We can't be all that bad." Sometimes we had tense moments. I never questioned my love for them, though. I asked God to let His love flow through me. That love is what would wake me up in the middle of the night, concerned that they might die without Christ. Finally, the day came when they could assure me that they were going to heaven and that they knew why. They were trusting, not in their own merit, but in the merit of Christ!

Conclusion

If God gave me a microphone with speakers that reached the entire world and told me I could say anything I wanted to Christians, I wouldn't *say* anything. I would *shout* eight words: "Let's start witnessing out of grace, not guilt!" Evangelism can become an enjoyable experience, not an endurable episode.

For that to happen, we must start looking at evangelism from God's perspective. It is a privilege, not a pain. He asks us to bring Christ to the lost; He will bring the lost to Christ. He's not asking us to push through closed doors, but to walk through open ones. His love can motivate us even in the midst of our fear.

After studying the Scriptures for more than thirty years, I'm convinced that our God of grace wants us to witness out of grace. He wants us to approach the lost with the excitement and anticipation evident in the words:

> *When I get to that beautiful city,*
> *And the saints all around me appear,*
> *I hope someone comes up to me and says,*
> *"You are the one who invited me here."*

QUESTIONS FOR REFLECTION

- How does guilt motivation hinder boldness in evangelism instead of encouraging it?

- Think of specific opportunities you've had to share the Gospel. In what ways can you see that you viewed them as a pain instead of a privilege?

- How does understanding that God only expects you to bring Christ to the lost and not the lost to Christ relieve some of the pressure of evangelism?

- In the past, how has fear in evangelism caused you to think unbiblically about the presence of His love in you toward lost people?

- How specifically should an understanding of the grace of God affect your attitude and thinking the next time you are presented with an opportunity to present the Gospel?

Chapter Nine

How to Regain a Heart
for Unbelievers

"When I came to Christ, I wanted to tell everybody about Him. He was the one person I felt all my friends needed to know, and I even saw one or two of them come to Christ. Yet now that I've been a Christian for ten years, I just don't have the same excitement for sharing Christ. I hate to admit it, but I really don't care whether I talk to unbelievers or not."

I've heard that kind of confession from more than one Christian. The confessions often range from not taking time to spend with unbelievers to not feeling concern about their eternal destiny. These Christians should be complimented for confessing something that's far easier to deny. Realizing their lack of compassion, they often ask: "How can I *regain* my concern for lost people?" A few simple, practical ideas can cause a world of change in regaining this concern for unbelievers.

Draw Closer to Jesus Christ

We must recognize that unconcern for unbelievers is—at least in part—a spiritual growth issue. If we take the Scriptures at face value, there is simply no way of getting close to Christ without seeing how much He cares for those for whom He died. Luke 19:10 is quite explicit: "For the Son of Man has come to seek and to save that which was lost." In light of that clear statement, is it possible to get close to the Master's heart without getting close to the Master's mission? Consider Matthew 4:19 where Christ extended the invitation, "Follow Me, and I will make you fishers of men." How, then, can we follow closely in His footsteps without being captivated by His concern for the lost? If we would like to think of ourselves as growing Christians, a good biblical barometer of our growth would be, "How concerned am I for lost people?"

Does that mean if we do not witness to one person a day, we are not close to Christ and have no concern for the lost? Not for a moment. He wants our lives to be motivated by relationships, not regulations. It is to say, however, that if we draw close to Jesus Christ, we will find His concern for the lost rubbing off on us.

It is like spending time with my friend in California who is an avid bass fisherman. Mention the subject of fishing around him and, regardless of the business pressures upon him, he comes alive. He'll tell you in a flash about the latest tournament, the latest lure, and the latest catch. I can't be with him very long without feeling like I'm missing out on something pretty exciting. I have to work on controlling my interest whenever I'm around him, lest he take me by my hand and lead me to the sporting goods store! Fishing isn't just fun for him—it's serious business.

Something similar happens when we get close to Christ. Known as the friend of sinners, His whole life revolved around lost people. Since they are so close to His heart, the closer we draw to Him, the closer we draw to the people for whom He died. Therefore, we ought to ask ourselves the question, "Are we spending the time daily getting to know Christ better, talking to Him through prayer, and letting Him talk to us through the Scriptures?" Or are we like Martha in Luke 10 who was so "worried and troubled about many things" that she neglected just sitting down and talking to Him and letting Him talk to her? A genuine, growing relationship with Him should lead to a growing closeness to non-Christians.

Spend Time with Unbelievers

Another way to regain concern for unbelievers is to examine our lives and make some necessary adjustments. Ask yourself this question: Am I living life in a cocoon? A Christian cocoon is any comfortable place that affords shelter from non-Christians. Once we come to know the Savior, our desires and interests have a way of changing. We still like the party life—but our parties are different. It's more enjoyable to be around believers and hear them speak of prayer, Bible study, or a bit of nourishment they have received through Christian radio. It's fun knowing those who realize there is more to life than a new house and a new car. Even church becomes a place of fellowship with Christians of like mind instead of our spending time with those of a different mind.

"But I'm not really comfortable around non-Christians," one might remark. But God never asks, "Are you comfortable around them?" God asks, "Do you pity them?" Jesus was moved with compassion for the multitudes that followed Him and longed to be their Shepherd and gather them into His fold (Matt. 9:36). If we share that compassion, we must spend time with lost people in hopes of leading them to the Savior.

If we are living in a Christian cocoon, we don't have contact with unbelievers. Without contacts, personal evangelism becomes impossible. How do we speak to people we never see?

Start listing non-Christians you know, even though you may have no meaningful contact with them. Then, considering a few at a time, think of ways you can cultivate a meaningful relationship with each one. Be realistic. You don't have any more time to give, so forget about taking time out of your schedule. Instead consider ways to work them into your schedule. A Friday night ball game at a local high school could be just as easily enjoyed with the company of an unbeliever. A non-Christian homemaker might welcome a ride to the mall. Bear in mind that even an hour together now might lead to an afternoon together later—and a superb opportunity to explain the grace of God proven on the cross.

Do you like to play tennis? Play it with a non-Christian. A man who was led to Christ said to me, "The good news is that I was led to Christ; the bad news is my tennis game is messed up." I asked the obvious question, "Why?" He replied, "The man God used to get me thinking about spiritual things prefers to play tennis with unbelievers, so I'll have to find a new tennis partner!" Do you know what else? The new believer respected his friend for that. He told me, "I understand. Frankly, I'd like to see him play tennis with as many non-Christians as possible, so he can have the impact on them that he had on me."

Ask God to Restore Your Concern for Non-Christians

Is God who He says or isn't He? Of course He is! If so, then we can speak to God as simply, humbly, and sincerely about our lack of concern for the lost as we speak about our temptations, financial struggles, employment hassles, or marital difficulties. The Scriptures exhort us, "Let us therefore come boldly to the throne of grace, that we may obtain mercy and find grace to help in time of need" (Heb. 4:16).

That being the case, I can come to Him and say, "God, You're easy to talk to, but what I want to tell You is not easy to talk about. I really don't share Your compassion for the lost. Quite frankly, non-Christians don't concern me that much. But if You will help me change, then I'm willing and I'd like to start today. Would You help me develop the same kind of heart that You have—one that cares for those who don't know You? I've seen You answer my other prayers. Would You kindly answer this one?" Or we can say, "I get my priorities so messed up, but if You will show me how, I want to move lost people up on my list of priorities."

One word of caution: If we sincerely mean what we pray, we need to stand back and get ready. God will answer. He has an abundant supply of compassion for those who ask Him for it.

First John 5:14–15 assures, "Now this is the confidence that we have in Him, that if we ask anything according to His will, He hears us. And if we know that He hears us, whatever we ask, we know that we have the petitions that we have asked of Him." There is no question that such a prayer is according to His will, so when we pray for a heart like His we may expect an answer.

As an evangelistic speaker, I get paid for speaking to the lost. I don't do it simply because I get paid to do it. I want to do it because one of the thrills of living is introducing lost people to Christ. If I find, then, that I am beginning to speak out of habit instead of concern, I have a good talk with the Lord. He has never failed to reignite in me a fire for unbelievers when I've come to Him in prayer. In fact, it's helped my understanding of Him and my prayer life a great deal. It's so comforting to know I can talk to Him about absolutely anything, and He won't embarrass me for asking; He'll just graciously answer. What a Father!

While I was speaking in the Midwest, a man introduced himself to me and shared a very interesting testimony. "A few weeks ago," he said, "I came face-to-face with the fact that I've lost a lot of my concern for unbelievers. I prayed and asked God to restore the concern I used to have. I didn't realize He would answer so quickly. The next day a co-worker asked me a question related to a spiritual issue. I immediately had an opportunity to talk about the Gospel." That simple conversation reminded the man how refreshing it is to talk with others about the Savior. God reignited his fire for sharing the Gospel.

Conclusion

If you are not where you need to be in your concern for lost people, put these principles in practice: Draw closer to Jesus Christ, spend time with unbelievers, and ask God to restore your concern for non-Christians.

Will you regain your concern for the lost overnight? Most likely, no. But in a matter of time, you'll find you're further along than you were. That in itself will begin to encourage you as you seek to have a heart closely aligned with God's. Remember, it's not just where you are but also the direction in which you're headed that's important. If six months from now you can say, "I have a much greater concern for lost people now than I did six months ago and here's the proof . . ." you will know you are on the right track.

QUESTIONS FOR REFLECTION

• Do you feel like you are growing in your spiritual walk with Christ?

• Look at the involvement you could have had with non-Christians over the last six months. How does the question "Do you pity them?" instead of "Are you comfortable around them?" affect future opportunities?

• How in our prayer life do we often become superficial instead of talking to God about specific needs and weaknesses in our lives?

• List several non-Christians you know. What can be done *now* to have the kind of meaningful contact with them that could result in conversations about Christ?

• As you think of your own conversion and the positive contacts Christians had with you, how should this encourage you to have the same kind of contact with the non-Christians you know?

Chapter Ten

How to Avoid Common
Mistakes in Evangelism

◈

Mark Twain is reported to have said, "I knew a man who grabbed a cat by the tail and learned forty percent more about cats than the man who didn't." There is no question about it. Experience is a *big* teacher through which one learns some extremely valuable lessons. I relish the story I read of a salesperson who was showing a doll to a father at Christmas. She explained, "This one really reminds you of little girls. When you lay her down, she closes her eyes and goes to sleep." With a skeptical look on his face, the father responded, "I gather from that comment that you've never had a little girl."

The same is true in evangelism. Experience teaches things one simply cannot learn any other way. One thing it teaches is how to avoid some common mistakes. After spending year after year interacting with non-Christians about the Gospel and interacting with believers about evangelism, I've discovered six mistakes that are worth discussing in some detail.

Mistake #1: Overlooking One of the Greatest Needs in Evangelism

Ask the average believer, "What is one of the greatest needs in evangelism?" and you will obtain a variety of answers: believers need to develop boldness in evangelism, Christians have too few non-Christian friends, we don't pray enough for people who are without Christ, we need to live Christlike lives in order to honor the Gospel, we need to get "on fire." Although all of these are extremely important and significant, there is an even greater need and that is a *clear* presentation of the Gospel. It is safe to say that multitudes have had the Gospel extended to them. It is also safe to say that a very small percentage of those have had the Gospel explained clearly. The Gospel, as Paul the apostle defines it in 1 Corinthians 15:3–4, is, "Christ died for our sins, and rose from the dead." The simple message of the Bible is the clearest message for the world.

How, specifically, has the message of the Gospel been misunderstood? Unbelievers often understand that Christ died. What they often miss when the Gospel is not made clear is that He died *for them!* It was on behalf of them, instead of them: a substitutionary kind of death. That is why it is absolutely free—no money down, nothing to pay later, satisfaction *guaranteed*. It is not that salvation doesn't cost, it is the fact that the cost has already been paid because Someone who was absolutely perfect died *in their place*. The price of saving them was paid two thousand years ago!

Take away that substitutionary death and one has taken away the meaning of the Gospel. The angels' announcement to the shepherds, as recorded in Luke 2:11, proclaimed, "For there is born to you this day in the city of David a Savior, who is Christ the Lord." The angels did not announce a Jesus who would die—that would not be a savior. They announced a Jesus who would die *in people's place*—a Savior!

In May of 1988, people throughout the United States were shocked and saddened at the news of the crash between a bus and a pickup truck which was going the wrong way on Interstate 71 in Kentucky. In a matter of seconds, the lives of twenty-seven young people returning from a youth camp were snuffed out. The nation was also struck when they heard of the sacrifice made by Joshua, one of the victims. He was about to jump from the exit of the bus when he saw his brother, Aaron, on the floor. With all the strength one musters at a time like that, he ran back, picked up his brother, and pushed him

80

out of the window. Joshua then died in the fiery explosion. He saved his brother by dying for him. He died in his place. Jesus Christ, the perfect Son of God, sacrificed His life in our place. Two thousand years ago, He died on a cross as our substitute and took the punishment we deserved. He then rose on the third day victorious over death and the Devil.

When Christ's substitutionary death is not presented clearly, some may receive the impression that Christ, by His death, merely opened the gates to heaven. The way to enter heaven, then, is by our good living and earnest deeds—a direct contradiction of Scripture. Eternal life is a free gift that comes through a *person*—that person being the one and only Jesus Christ, God's perfect sacrifice. Jesus' rebuke to those of His day was, "But you are not willing to come to Me that you may have life" (John 5:40).

One of the single greatest needs in evangelism is for a *clear* presentation of the Gospel. When the Gospel is made clear, a person comes to understand something so awesome that he or she is caused to echo what someone once said to me, "That has to be the most beautiful thing I have ever heard."

Mistake #2: Assuming People Know What Saving Faith Is

Another question that generates a variety of responses is, What is saving faith? People have answered that it is surrender, commitment, belief, dependence, getting right with God, hope, acceptance, or conviction about something. But what exactly does the Bible mean when it says, "Therefore, having been justified by faith, we have peace with God through our Lord Jesus Christ" (Rom. 5:1). Jesus said, "Most assuredly, I say to you, he who believes in Me has everlasting life" (John 6:47). Simply put, saving faith means admitting we are sinners, recognizing that Jesus Christ, God's perfect Son, died in our place and rose again, and placing our *trust* in Him alone to save us—not in our good deeds or religious efforts, not in the church we attend, or baptism—but in Christ *alone* to save us.

In June of 1991 the *Buffalo News* told of a boy weighing two hundred pounds who was drowning in the Allegheny River. He was clinging to a small vine about one hundred and fifty yards downstream from the beginning of a five hundred-yard-long retaining wall and was about to go under. A woman weighing only one hundred and twenty pounds slid down the sixty degree embankment, leapt into the river, and swam to him. She told him to roll onto his back and pulled him upstream. All he could do was trust her to save him, which she did. Similarly, we must trust in Christ alone as our only way to heaven. We must depend on Him alone to save us.

When people do not understand saving faith, several things happen. One is that they know *about* God, but they don't *know* God and are not related to Him. For that reason we are plainly told in John 1:12, "But as many as received Him, to them He gave the right to become children of God, to those who *believe* in His name." While flying home from Seoul, Korea, in September of 1996, God in His kindness placed me next to a man who, searching and sympathetic to spiritual things, had begun studying the Bible. When I shared with him the Bad News/Good News, I was careful to point out that one is not saved unless one's trust is in Christ alone for salvation. The understanding of saving faith was something he had not had before. Before we departed, he assured me that his trust was now in Christ alone as his only way to heaven.

Another misunderstanding of saving faith is when people graduate from trusting their works to save them, to trusting Christ *and* their works. This is not saving faith. When Christ died on the cross, His proclamation was, "It is finished!" (John 19:30). He meant that He had done everything that could be done to accomplish our salvation. Nothing was left undone. He did not proclaim, "I have helped you," or "It is partially completed." Instead, "It is finished." *Therefore, the meaning of saving faith is that we have to be satisfied with the thing that satisfies God.* Since God was pleased with His Son's death in our place, when we come to God trusting His Son alone to save us we are forever His.

Another very dangerous thing that happens when people do not understand what saving faith means is that they have "faith in faith" instead of faith in Christ. By "faith in faith" I mean faith in a dogma, the set of beliefs established by the church, a system and schedule of participating in religious observances, rules or principles of conduct believers are expected to live by, or a satisfactory performance in their own mind and the conviction their lives are indeed God-honoring lives. As I once said to an audience, "Some of you *have* faith. You have faith God is going to keep your car running. You have faith He is going to keep your children healthy. You have faith He's going to provide your groceries. And you are convinced that by faith in your faith (I mean by that the God-honoring life you are trying to live) you are going to get to heaven. God is asking you to trust *Christ* as your only way to heaven. He's asking you to put faith in a *Person*." One who trusted Christ that night told me, "I've never understood that before. You're right. I do trust God to keep my children healthy and do trust Him to keep my car running. And I thought that through faith in my faith—my life of dependence on God for my physical needs—I'd get to heaven. I never knew I had to trust Christ to save me."

We dare not assume people understand what saving faith is because most don't. It is so uncharacteristic of people in our society to place simple trust in anyone or anything. It is an amazing thing that through simple trust in a Person as our only way to heaven, we will receive an absolutely free gift, especially one so great as eternal life. For that reason, we must, as I've said for so many years, "Be clear! Be clear! Be clear!"

Mistake #3: Assuming Anyone's Salvation

Christian has become to many the same thing as *Republican* or *Democrat*. It simply identifies a class of people. How one gets into this class is not always clear to many, although most believe that attendance at a church on a Sunday morning is an absolute requirement. After all, how can one expect to darken the gates of heaven if they have not darkened the doors of a church?

The term *born again* also leaves people completely confused. I was most surprised some years ago as I watched the news of a hurricane just off the coast of the United States that was reported to have been born again. I never realized that a hurricane can have a spiritual experience!

For that reason, it would be a mistake to assume anyone's salvation. A person may have never understood the Gospel—Christ died for our sins and arose—and he or she may have never understood the meaning of saving faith—trust in Christ alone. The fact is that many are insecure about their salvation and would confess this if not for the embarrassment they feel. It is sometimes easier to confess this insecurity to a stranger than a friend. I do not know how many people have pulled me aside, away from the hearing of their pastor or friend, to say to me, "I've been going to this church for years but this is the first time I've ever understood that eternal life is a free gift that comes through trust in Christ alone to save." A person in Wisconsin where I spoke recently approached me at the end of the service and said, "I want you to know I trusted Christ this morning. I told people I became a Christian in my twenties. But I have never understood what you told us today." I later learned that she was a source of concern to many who felt that although her spiritual interest and zeal were to be commended, she most likely did not understand the simple plan of salvation. Interestingly enough, God used me as the voice of a stranger to penetrate her mind and soul.

For these reasons we are wise to ask people two questions: (1) When you die, do you know if you are going straight to heaven, and (2) If you were to stand before God and He were to ask you, "Why should I let you into heaven?" what would you tell Him? Their answers will tell you where they stand on their understanding of saving faith in Christ alone.

Mistake #4: Letting Satan Convince You "That's What They Are All Like"

When you step out to evangelize, you will not meet individuals who are open doors of opportunity every time. Sometimes you will meet individuals who are like unbudgeable boulders. The individual's response may range from not interested to absolutely angry that you would address spiritual things. That person may ask questions so pointless as "Could God create a rock so big He couldn't lift it?" to questions so reasonable as "If God is a God of love, why are there starving people in the world?" It may be an individual who is very bitter against God because of a tragedy in his or her family, or someone who is convinced that he or she is God Himself. Satan often uses such "hard cases" to say, in essence, "That is what they're all like. Evangelizing is just a waste of time on your part."

These individuals do exist. Jesus alerted His disciples to them when He said, "And whoever will not receive you nor hear your words, when you depart from that house or city, shake off the dust from your feet. Assuredly, I say to you, it will be more tolerable for the land of Sodom and Gomorrah in the day of judgment than for that city!" (Matt. 10:14–15).

I too have met them. One time a man said to me in complete sincerity and mockery, "I don't believe in Jesus Christ. If when I die, I find out He is for real, it will be a one-on-one fight between Him and me. If I win, I'll send Him to hell. If He wins, He can send me there." These "hard cases" are few and far between, but Satan tries to convince us that that's what they are all like. Although in the pit of our stomach we know that's not true, Satan becomes a master of intimidation.

Three things when linked together solve the problem of intimidation—obedience, determination, and experience. All three cause us to do one thing—talk to another, then another, then another about the Good News of Christ. In so doing we meet those who *are* the norm; those who are willing to talk about spiritual things when approached with politeness and sensitivity, to those who are like fruit that is so ripe for the Gospel it is about to fall off the limb. We meet people who are similar to the ones Christ described in John 4:35 when He said, "Do you not say, 'There are still four months and then comes the harvest'? Behold, I say to you, lift up your eyes and look at the fields, for they are already white for harvest!"

That's why evangelistic people keep being evangelistic—they know how open and receptive most people are. When they meet one who isn't, they recognize that person as the exception, not the norm. Certainly, people vary extensively, but I have witnessed firsthand more open and interested people than unbudgeable ones.

Mistake #5: Assuming You Will Either Succeed or Fail in Evangelism

Evangelizing is a learning experience. Each time we share Christ with someone we are that much wiser how to do it. Instead of looking at it as a learning experience, we sometimes classify each incident as a success or a failure. The differentiation we feel is very clear—successes are those times when we lead others to Christ and failures are those times when we don't.

The problem is self-created and unbiblical. First of all, God is responsible for results. A verse believers ought to have firmly planted in their minds as they evangelize is the one I keep going back to: John 6:44, "No one can come to Me unless the Father who sent Me draws him." Referring to the results in spiritual ministry, Paul the apostle testified, "Who then is Paul, and who is Apollos, but ministers through whom you believed, as the Lord gave to each one? I planted, Apollos watered, but God gave the increase. So then neither he who plants is anything, nor he who waters, but God who gives the increase" (1 Cor. 3:5–7).

God is clearly in control. With that in mind, He uses us in different ways with different people. We may be the one who gets a non-Christian thinking about spiritual things, the one who *continues* her thinking, the one who leads her to Christ, or the one who helps at *any* point along that line. Jesus' comforting words in evangelism were, "One sows and another reaps" (John 4:37).

But what about the times we have had an opportunity for presenting the Gospel and neglected to take advantage of it? Or the times we did not handle an opportunity as well as we could have? Have we failed? First of all, if in disobedience we did not reach out with the Gospel, we have failed to take advantage of what may have been a God-given opportunity. But upon confession, God writes "forgiven" over us, not "failure." Should we not handle an opportunity as well as we could have, have we not learned from it and has not God taught us something from it? If so, that is a tremendous success—we learned something that will be of immense value with our next opportunity.

There are missed opportunities and in that sense "failures" to take advantage of opportunity. But I know of no person Christ ever called a "failure" in evangelism. God is a God of grace. His concern is that we follow Him and allow Him to *make* us fishers of men (Matt. 4:19). If we will do the learning, He'll do the teaching.

Mistake #6: Entertaining the Notion That Only Walking Bible Encyclopedias Reach People for Christ

Ask a believer the question, "What hinders you in evangelism?" and one response will come up repeatedly: "I'm afraid I will not be able to answer their questions and objections." They are referring to the statements non-Christians make such as, "I don't believe the Bible." "Christians are hypocrites." "I don't believe there is a God." "Christ was not who He said He was." Immediately, a believer begins to think that in order to evangelize, he or she must be a walking Bible encyclopedia—a person who can refute any argument, answer any question, explain any verse, and respond to any objection a non-Christian raises.

If we look at the examples of evangelism in the Bible and in this present day, we can see that the notion of having to be a Bible encyclopedia is a mistake. When Paul entered Corinth—a city filled with intellectuals and philosophers—he said, "And I, brethren, when I came to you, did not come with excellence of speech or of wisdom declaring to you the testimony of God. For I determined not to know anything among you except Jesus Christ and Him crucified" (1 Cor. 2:1–2). Three verses later, he explained why—"that your faith should not be in the wisdom of men but in the power of God."

Paul recognized what is so easily forgotten in evangelism. An argument can be answered with an argument, logic can be answered with logic, and persuasion can be responded to with persuasion. But in order for conviction to occur, in order for faith to be real, God has to take the truth of the Gospel, drive it home to a lost person's heart, and cause him or her to come to Him in faith. Paul wanted no one to respond saying, "I believe because Paul convinced me," but everyone to respond saying, "I believe because *God* convinced me." His concern was that nobody respond, "What a brilliant speaker!" Instead, it was that everyone respond, "What a beautiful Savior." Study Paul's approach in Athens as recorded in a Acts 17:16–34 and one finds a similar thing to be true—he entered the city not as a Bible encyclopedia who could respond to every question or argument, but as a proclaimer of the Good News of Christ's death and resurrection.

Now let's look at present day examples. What group of people wins more to Christ than anyone else? Are they students in a Bible-teaching seminary? Although there are students who are most fervent and faithful, as a class of individuals they are not the ones who win the most to Christ. Are they the leaders of the local churches? One would hope that would be the case, but it isn't. Are they the mature believers who know the Bible like the back of their hand? Once more, there are such believers, but as a class of people they wouldn't win the prize for evangelistic fervor.

Instead, it's the new believers—the people one day, one week, one month, or one year old in Christ. They are so thrilled that their eternal destiny has been instantaneously changed, so grateful for the miracle God made out of their "mess," they are compelled to tell someone, to tell anybody the good news of the Gospel. What is quite interesting, though, is that they often know very little more than the simple salvation message which they tell to another after another after another.

Biblically and practically, it's proven. One does not need to be a Bible encyclopedia. One desperately needs to be a willing instrument in the Savior's hands. As with so many things, it's the issue of the heart, not the issue of the head, that makes the difference.

Conclusion

An individual once commented, "Experience is a valuable teacher. It helps you recognize a mistake when you do it again." Mistakes, though, don't have to be repeated. Learning how to avoid these six common mistakes can make a tremendous difference in evangelism. It's no wonder the book of Proverbs speaks of the wisdom that comes with age. How else can one learn experience? There is, though, only two things we can do with experience—pass through it or learn from it. For those who simply pass through it, they learn nothing. For those who learn from it, they become immensely rich—rich in the thing that brings tremendous satisfaction and eternal results—representing the King of Kings to the lost.

QUESTIONS FOR REFLECTION

- As you contemplate opportunities to evangelize, what examples or illustrations can you think of that will help you clearly communicate the Gospel and the meaning of saving faith?

- Can you think of individuals whose salvation you have assumed when it would have been proper to engage in conversation to determine whether they really understood the Gospel?

- In what ways have you let a negative experience in evangelism discourage you from talking to more people?

- In what specific ways does a biblical understanding of faithfulness versus failure increase boldness in evangelism?

- As you have grown as a Christian and increased your knowledge of the Bible, are there ways you have allowed your presentation of the Gospel to become more confusing to the non-Christian?

Chapter Eleven

How to Encourage
New Believers to Grow

Believers have their faults. Just ask the people who live with them! But one thing for which many of them ought to be commended is that they have a very conscientious concern for new Christians. They do not want to introduce a person to Christ and simply leave them there; they want to see them grow in grace. That becomes such a concern at times it even hinders them from evangelizing. They explain, "If I lead someone to Christ, I feel I have a responsibility to help him or her grow. But where in the world do I find the time? I don't have enough time for everything that is on my plate right now."

Before we delve into what Scripture says in this area, two items may be stressed. For one, don't take God's responsibility on your shoulders. If you allow God to do so, He will show you where to take some *thing* out of your schedule to work *someone*—the new convert—into your schedule. It is amazing how God helps us make the necessary adjustments when our priorities have become the same as His. Furthermore, if for any reason you lead someone to Christ and can't disciple him or her as you wish, God in His grace and sovereignty can bring along someone else who can. Examine the ministry of Paul the apostle. There were nearly forty individuals who worked with him in follow-up. It takes the entire body of Christ and not just one individual to get the job accomplished. Just as God often uses more than one person to bring someone to Christ, God often uses many different people to help him or her grow.

A second item cannot be stressed enough. Please don't misunderstand. I as much as anyone want to see new converts grow. That's why our organization has tried to be very diligent in extending as much assistance in follow-up as possible to the local churches as they disciple those who come to Christ in our outreaches. But even if they should not grow as we would like, don't ever overlook the fact that their eternal destiny has been changed—solely by the grace of God. If they have sincerely trusted Christ, they will not spend eternity forever separated from God. To have any less of a perspective would be to downplay the tremendous transaction that takes place the moment a person is saved and thereby transferred from the kingdom of darkness into the kingdom of light.

With these stated, how *do* we encourage new believers to grow? How do we encourage them to be people who enter the front door of a church and become leaders, instead of people who simply enter through the front door and walk out the back? New converts need to hear us saying to them loudly and clearly three things.

You're Not Just Part of God's Family, You're Part of Mine

In Paul's mind when people became children of God, they not only became part of God's family, they became part of his. He reminded the new converts of Thessalonica, "But we were gentle among you, just as a nursing mother cherishes her own children" (1 Thess. 2:7). The text there means what it says. Paul explained that the way a nursing mother takes care of a child was the way he took care of them. He repeated that emphasis four verses later when he said, "As you know how we exhorted, and comforted, and charged every one of you, as a father does his own children" (1 Thess. 2:11). They were not simply the children of God, they were also the children of Paul.

Rest assured that to be part of God's family was never a minor thing with Paul. The *majesty* in Paul's mind of what happens the moment one trusts Christ is evident when he says, "He has delivered us from the power of darkness and conveyed us into the kingdom of the Son of His love, in whom we have redemption through His blood, the forgiveness of sins" (Col. 1:13–14). They were God's children, that was for sure. But they were also his children to nurture and care for the way a parent does his own.

That attitude must permeate the relationship we have with new believers. They are not simply "new converts," they are children who have entered God's family and into ours as well. Along these lines, children are individuals. Each one is unique and has his or her own idiosyncrasies, weaknesses, and strengths. That is one reason they must be discipled one-on-one. Putting a new believer into a "class of new converts" is not sufficient to see each one grow properly. One has temptations in one area that another doesn't. One came from a drug background where religion was unheard of, while another came from a religious background where drugs were unheard of. One is in his late teens, approaching college, while another is in her late fifties, approaching retirement. Gender alone makes their circumstances and situations differ.

Just as individuals in a human family are not treated as a class but as individuals, people in God's family must be treated as individuals. God does not produce His people from a copier, He carved each one with His own hand.

Take My Hand and Let Me Lead You

People are forgetful. How many times have you heard the expression, "I'd forget my own head if it were not screwed on." Because we are so forgetful, we fail to remember where we were spiritually at the time we came to Christ.

If we clearly understood the Gospel, we knew we were going to heaven when we died. What we were not certain about was where to go on earth while yet living. What exactly do we do after we come to Christ? How often I have heard the comment, "When I came to Christ, I never knew there was anything else to do. I never knew there was such a thing as growing as a Christian."

Paul's approach to new Christians was never "Lots of luck—go for it." Go for what? Instead, his approach was "Take my hand and let me lead you."

That meant two things. Paul first had to know what goal he had in mind for them. Otherwise, it would be the blind leading the blind. One cannot lead a person without knowing where to head. Interestingly enough, Paul's goal was never simply to get the individual within the doors of church or even to persuade them of the need to complete a ten-week study course. Church attendance and study courses may well be important, but to Paul they would have only been the means, not the end. Instead, his goal was to produce mature disciples of Jesus Christ.

Paul testified in Colossians 1:28, "Him we preach, warning every man and teaching every man in all wisdom, that we may present every man perfect in Christ Jesus." The word *perfect* has the idea of mature. He wished them to be so mature that they could be, as he explained in Titus 2, older men teaching younger men and older women teaching younger women how to live for Christ. In so doing, they would demonstrate the kind of character needed to be leaders in a local church.

Secondly, he had to impart direction to them. That is, if they were going to reach maturity he had to explain to them *how* to live for Christ. He did just that, "Finally then, brethren, we urge and exhort in the Lord Jesus that you should abound more and more, just as you received from us *how* you ought to walk and please God; for you know what commandments we gave you through the Lord Jesus" (1 Thess. 4:1–2).

One can imagine how helpful that was to the new converts of Thessalonica. The Gospel so spread in Thessalonica that we are told not only did some Jews come to Christ but also "a great multitude of the devout Greeks, and not a few of the leading women, joined Paul and Silas" (Acts 17:4). Some of these were saved from a heathen, idol worshiping background (1 Thess. 1:9). They only knew how to worship a god who didn't exist, not walk with a God who does exist. Although Thessalonica never had a reputation for immorality like Corinth had, immoral practices were common and often were carried out in the name of religion. Coming out of that background, the new converts needed to know, "Where do I go from here?"

A new convert cannot simply be told, "Now grow as a Christian." They must be shown *how* with an attitude that says, "Take my hand and let me lead you." That is one of the many things that must have prompted Dawson Trotman, founder of the Navigators, whose life was burdened for evangelism and the growth of new converts, to say, "Follow-up is not done by something, it is done by *someone*."

We must emphasize that maturity is the goal and new Christians must see us growing toward maturity as well. Otherwise we confuse them immensely by telling them to head in one direction while we are headed in another. Paul was very effective in discipling new converts because he too was headed toward the same goal. His clear testimony in Philippians 3:12–15 was,

> Not that I have already attained, or am already perfected; but I press on, that I may lay hold of that for which Christ Jesus has also laid hold of me. Brethren, I do not count myself to have apprehended; but one thing I do, forgetting those things which are behind and reaching forward to those things which are ahead, I press toward the goal for the prize of the upward call of God in Christ Jesus. Therefore let us, as many as are mature, have this mind; and if in anything you think otherwise, God will reveal even this to you.

We often like to take the words "forgetting the things which are behind" as referring to Paul's past sins for which he asked the Lord's forgiveness. Undoubtedly Paul knew that what was no longer on God's mind did not need to be on his. In context, he is referring to his past spiritual accomplishments. Paul was never satisfied with where he was spiritually. He always wanted more. Concerning the issue of who should disciple another, it is not how long the discipler has been a Christian or how much he or she knows; it is whether or not the discipler is a *growing* Christian headed toward the goal of maturity.

We dare not give the new convert the idea that the goal is, "Now since you're a Christian, God expects all new Christians to go to church." True, believers ought to welcome the opportunity to worship with other believers and as Hebrews 10:25 admonishes, forsake not "the assembling of ourselves together." But attendance in a Bible-believing church is a means, not an end. Viewed as an end, one can go there and be as dead as a telephone pole—and just about as replaceable. Viewed as a means, it becomes a way to learn how to live a Christlike life and to encourage others along the same path to maturity. To get new Christians started, we ought to be taking them to church with us and introducing them to a new circle of friends with whom they can enjoy the Christian life.

"Take my hand and let me lead you" means we must explain to

them how to pray and how to study the Scriptures. Communication is key to growth. That is true in any and every relationship. A husband and wife do not grow close if they do not communicate. Two people do not become good friends apart from communication. Similarly, a new believer does not draw close to his Savior without communication. They must speak to the Savior through prayer and let the Savior speak to them through the Scriptures. But if they are not shown how and where to begin their study of Scriptures, the results could be most unfortunate. They may begin in Genesis and get discouraged trying to understand the genealogies or in Revelation and become discouraged trying to understand what's going to happen when. I recently met with a man who wants very much to be all he can be spiritually. But he's frustrated that nobody has ever shown him how to study the Bible.

I recommend to new converts that they begin with Philippians. Philippians is the easiest book of the entire Bible for a new Christian to understand and it talks about Christian living on a day by day, week by week basis. I recommend they study that book for a month, reading a chapter a day. Since Philippians only has four chapters, they should start over with chapter one on the fifth day. They will see things the second time through the book that they didn't see the first, and the fourth time see things they didn't see the third. I always remind them not to worry about the verses they don't understand, but those they do. Upon completing Philippians, they can then go to the books that follow, staying in each book for a month. After each study which allows God to speak to them, they can then speak to God in prayer as a friend speaks to a friend. I explained to one new convert, "Don't worry about using fancy words or religious sounding language, just talk to God the way you would to a friend." I'll never forget her priceless words as she prayed, "Dear God, this is Sarah. It's been a long time since you've heard from me. But we are going to be talking a lot more in the coming weeks!" How exciting it was to hear such a heart to heart talk that a new child of God was having with her heavenly Father.

"Take my hand and let me lead you" is a New Testament approach and is essential if new Christians are to know where to head spiritually and how to get there.

I'll Do Whatever It Takes

What did Paul mean when he said to the Thessalonians, "You know how we exhorted, and comforted, and charged every one of you" (1 Thess. 2:11)? The three verbs in this verse represent the idea that Paul laid before them a particular course of conduct, urged them to pursue it, and gave them the necessary comfort and encouragement they needed as they were doing so. Paul was basically saying to his new converts, "I'll do whatever it takes."

Paul was well aware that the new Christians of Thessalonica would face persecution. He himself had experienced deep hatred from the Thessalonian Jews who hounded him all the way to Berea. Could those who had embraced his message and his Savior experience any less? So what did he do? With an "I'll do whatever it takes" attitude, he sent his companion Timothy back to them. He explained,

> Therefore, when we could no longer endure it, we thought it good to be left in Athens alone, and sent Timothy, our brother and minister of God, and our fellow laborer in the gospel of Christ, to establish you and encourage you concerning your faith, that no one should be shaken by these afflictions; for you yourselves know that we are appointed to this. For, in fact, we told you before when we were with you that we would suffer tribulation, just as it happened, and you know. For this reason, when I could no longer endure it, I sent to know your faith, lest by some means the tempter had tempted you, and our labor might be in vain (1 Thess. 3:1–5).

Even the words Paul used to depict what it took to help new converts achieve maturity in Christ represents a "whatever it takes, I'll do it" attitude. After explaining his desire to present every person mature in Christ, he says in Colossians 1:29, "To this end I also labor, striving according to His working which works in me mightily." *Labor* depicts work that could be exhausting. Although a tiring task at times, Paul was willing and ready to do whatever it took to see them become mature in the Savior.

Paul's "doing whatever it takes" mentality started on his knees because of how persistently he prayed for them. To cite just one example when he spoke of how he prayed for the new converts of Ephesus, we read,

> Therefore I also, after I heard of your faith in the Lord Jesus and your love for all the saints, do not cease to give thanks for you, making mention of you in my prayers: that the God of our Lord Jesus Christ, the Father of glory, may give to you the spirit of wisdom and revelation in the knowledge of Him, the eyes of your understanding being enlightened; that you may know what is the hope of His calling, what are the riches of the glory of His inheritance in the saints, and what is the exceeding greatness of His power toward us who believe, according to the working of His mighty power which He worked in Christ when He raised Him from the dead and seated Him at His right hand in the heavenly places, far above all principality and power and might and dominion, and every name that is named, not only in this age but also in that which is to come. And He put all things under His feet, and gave Him to be head over all things to the church, which is His body, the fullness of Him who fills all in all (Eph. 1:15–23).

Simply put, he wanted them to continue the course they had begun and grow in their knowledge of Christ. To that end he prayed and kept on praying.

Life is a matter of priorities. Paul was clear to the Thessalonian Christians that they were high on his list of priorities. So committed was he that each missionary journey he took increased in length by at least one year as he went back to visit the people and confirm churches in at least nine of the places he evangelized.

An "I'll do whatever it takes" mentality is critical to seeing new Christians grow. But as noted earlier, such an approach demands an expenditure in two areas—time and energy. Time-wise, it often takes far longer to see new converts grow than it does to see them come to Christ. Just as physical children don't grow overnight, neither do spiritual children. Dawson Trotman once said, "You can lead a soul to Christ in from twenty minutes to a couple of hours. But it takes from twenty weeks to a couple of years to get him on the road to maturity." Energy-wise, follow-up of new converts can also be demanding. It takes energy to help mend marriages, assist in the rearranging of priorities, help them desert bad habits and master good ones, and help them become responsible, productive members of the body of Christ. I've become far more weary discipling new converts than I ever have become leading people to Christ. In short, follow-up can be exhausting.

As a bare minimum, a new believer needs a discipler to meet with him a minimum of once a week for eight weeks. Should the discipling continue for a longer period, that will be even more helpful. But those first eight weeks are when a new convert sometimes has his or her greatest adjustments, greatest temptations, and greatest doubts. To have a brother or sister in Christ meeting with the new convert can make a marked difference. Should the new convert feel a bit threatened by an eight week suggestion, one needs the patience to take it one week at a time, giving the new Christian time to adjust to the kind of relationship he or she has never known.

Such follow-up is admittedly demanding but the results make it worth it all. To see them one day stand before the Lord, trophies of His grace to be abundantly rewarded, will be all the "payback" needed. That thought was a most exhilarating one to Paul as he said in 1 Thessalonians 2:19–20, "For what is our hope, or joy, or crown of rejoicing? Is it not even you in the presence of our Lord Jesus Christ at His coming? For you are our glory and joy." With this in mind, as new Christians were a priority with Paul, they need to be a priority with us.

That explains, though, why each new believer must be given individual attention. What it takes for one new believer to grow will not necessarily be the same for another. Once more they are not a "class of converts," they are new Christians individually Spirit-produced and handwoven by the Almighty God.

What if you want to help, but simply don't have the time? As I mentioned earlier, follow-up is ultimately the job of the body of Christ. First Corinthians 12 and Ephesians 4 are explicit that God has equipped believers in different ways so that together we might accomplish the needed tasks. The body of Christ is not one, it is many. Did not Paul make use of Timothy? Should one person not have the needed time to disciple a new convert, somebody else in the church does. But may I stress again, we ought *also* to ask ourselves, "Why do I not have the time or energy?" If it is due to justifiable reasons, fine. But should it be due to the fact that *things* are more important than people, it's time to rearrange our priorities. After all, people are part of the permanent. Things are part of the passing.

Conclusion

Encouraging new believers to grow is not rocket science. It amounts to people being concerned about people and has to do with attitude as much as action. There are three accusations the Thessalonians never could have made of Paul. They never could have said, "He didn't care what happened to me after I came to Christ," "He never showed me how to grow as a Christian," or "When I needed him he wasn't there." Instead the three thoughts that continually characterized his approach to new believers were, "You're not just part of God's family, you're part of mine," "Take my hand and let me lead you," and "I'll do whatever it takes." As we think of our own approach to new Christians, we would do well to ask, "Has my attitude and approach been the same as Paul's?"

What if with even a believer's willingness to exemplify these ideas, the new Christian shows no response and no desire to do his or her part? Paul never exempted anyone from their personal responsibilities. Should the new believer have no desire to grow we need not say, "There is little if anything we can do." We can fervently *pray* that God will work in a new convert's life to show him or her the need to follow the admonition in 2 Peter 3:18, "Grow in the grace and knowledge of our Lord and Savior Jesus Christ." In light of the fact that we are speaking to an Almighty God, those prayers are not a small thing. The God who loves all and desires a close relationship with His children has His own ways of awakening them to their needs, causing them to be dissatisfied with where they are spiritually and to embark on a path of continual growth. Even our prayers are an essential part of follow-up.

QUESTIONS FOR REFLECTION

- How specifically does the *mentality* with which we approach new Christians affect our approach in working with them?

- How is the phrase "people need example, not just exhortation" true in helping new believers grow in Christ?

- In what specific ways is evangelism sometimes easier than follow-up?

- How have your personal priorities aided or hindered you in assisting in the discipleship of new believers?

- How can concerns about follow-up not looked at in a biblical way hinder you in personal evangelism?

Chapter Twelve

How to Help Those Who Struggle with Salvation

Agony, terror, frustration, and hopelessness were all written across her face. Should I live to be one hundred, I doubt that I will ever forget her expression or her words. She repeated them twice although once would have been enough. She confessed, "I have always struggled with my salvation. I've heard you have helped others in this area. If you can't help me, I'm going to commit suicide. I'm tired of living not knowing for sure if I'm saved."

One could certainly wonder, "Why in the world would one who is not certain they are saved ever consider suicide?" The logic behind that escapes me as well. One thing for certain, although she may be the extreme, there are many like her who struggle with whether or not they are saved. What they are going through can be simply stated—while fearing the possibility of death in hell, they are meanwhile living in hell on earth. The reason is understandable. I don't know of anything more frightening than wanting to go to heaven and not being certain you will.

How do you help those who struggle with their salvation? How can you bring them to that delightful experience of knowing they are God's and knowing why? How can you bring them to that point of being as certain of heaven as though they are already there?

Rest assured, God wants every believer to experience that kind of certainty. In 1 John 5:13 we are plainly told, "These things I have written to you who believe in the name of the Son of God, that you may know that you have eternal life." The word *know* there has the idea to know *absolutely*. As certain as we are of our address on earth, we ought to be just as certain of what our address will be one second after we die.

Having spoken to many who struggled with their salvation, I have found that there is not one reason people struggle with their salvation. There are at least four. You must first determine why a person is struggling in order to discover how to help him or her.

There Are Those Who Have Never Understood the Gospel

There are those who have every reason to doubt their salvation because they have never been saved. They have never understood the Gospel.

There are some things in the Bible that are extremely difficult to understand. But there are some things in the Bible extremely difficult to misunderstand, such as the freeness of God's grace.

The one book of the Bible written specifically for non-Christians is the Gospel of John. We know that because the person God used to write it claimed that as his purpose. In John 20:31 we read, "But these are written that you may believe that Jesus is the Christ, the Son of God, and that believing you may have life in His name." There is no way one could read the Gospel of John without hearing the same message over and over again. That message is the one Christ reduced to eight words when He said, "He who believes in Me has everlasting life" (John 6:47). Five chapters later, He repeated this same message when He said to a person grieving over a deceased brother, "I am the resurrection and the life. He who believes in Me, though he may die, he shall live. And whoever lives and believes in Me shall never die" (John 11:25–26).

We have to come to God as we are, sinners deserving of hell. We must recognize that Jesus Christ as the perfect Son of God died in our place on a cross taking the punishment we deserved.

The *Dallas Morning News* in July of 1993 told of a couple married for less than a year who were at the law firm where the husband was employed. The wife, an attorney at another law firm, planned to study until her husband's shift ended. As she settled into an empty thirty-third floor office, her husband burst in and yelled, "You've got to get out, they've heard shots!" Immensely frightened, they found another empty office and attempted to hide behind a file cabinet. Unfortunately, the gunman found them. The wife was wounded in her right arm and chest but escaped death because her twenty-eight-year-old husband wrapped his body around hers and died in her place. The gunman killed eight people and wounded six others before committing suicide.

Similarly, Jesus Christ took the punishment we deserved and died as our substitute. He took the punishment for our sins. The nails that should have been driven through our hands were driven through His. The third day He arose victorious over sin and death. It is for that precise reason God can extend eternal life as a free gift. The price for our sin has already been paid. Jesus Christ paid it by His own death and resurrection.

How, though, do we receive that free gift? The word the Gospel of John echoes ninety-eight times is *believe*. It simply means that by recognizing that Christ died as my substitute, I am *trusting* Him alone as my only way to heaven. That is, I am agreeing with Christ about His own atoning death when He declared, "It is finished!" (John 19:30). When we place our trust in Christ alone to save us, we recognize that *nothing* in and of ourselves make us worthy of heaven. At that point, the greatest transaction ever to occur takes place as God considers our sins covered underneath the blood shed on the cross. At the same time the term *justify* in the Bible explains to us that God places His Son's righteousness upon us in such a way that when God looks upon us, He no longer sees our sins but instead sees the perfection of His Son, Jesus Christ. Romans 4:5 announces the results of such a transaction by declaring, "But to him who does not work but believes on Him who justifies the ungodly, his faith is accounted for righteousness."

That message—that one is simply saved by trusting Christ—is so simple that *millions* have missed it. Why? One huge reason is that we are so accustomed to working for or earning everything we have, one's immediate thought is that the only way to heaven is to work hard, do good, live right, and obey God. Ask the average person if she thinks she is going to heaven, she'll respond in words such as "I think I have a good shot at it." Ask her why, she'll respond, "I live a whole lot better than most people I know." God's standard, though, is not a neighbor, a preacher, or a pope; it's His Son. Alongside of Him, every person alive is a gross sinner deserving of hell. God can only accept us based on His Son's death, not on the basis of our deeds.

Because so many have missed the message of the free gift of God through personal trust in Christ to save them, they are uncertain of their salvation. Their uncertainty is understandable. If people could only get to heaven on the basis of their good deeds, the question would forever linger over their heads, "How good is good enough?" Such people lack the certainty of their salvation because they are unbelievers. They have every right to be uncertain!

Along the same lines, there are those who "graduate" from trusting their works to save them to trusting Christ *and* their good works. They, too, are unbelievers. The message of the Gospel is that we must agree with God about His Son. His Son did not make the *down* payment for our sins. Instead, He made the *full* payment. His words were, "It is finished." We must come to God, so trusting in the person of Christ to save us, that we recognize that if He cannot save us, we are absolutely without any doubt or hope going to hell. As I have explained to many, salvation is not Christ plus, but Christ period!

A noted Christian leader of years past is reported to have told some students, "If when I stand before God He asks me, 'Why should I let you in heaven?' I am going to say, 'Because Jesus Christ died for me.'" He then continued, "If at that time God says to me, 'I am sorry, that is not enough,' all I am going to do is walk away because that is all I have!"

That is salvation. Coming to God as a sinner, recognizing He died for us and arose, and trusting Him to save us. Because some have missed that message, they are without Christ and without eternal life. The struggle over their salvation will only be resolved by coming to Christ in simple faith receiving His free gift of life eternal.

For that reason, such people must be asked the question, "Do you know if you were to die you'd go to heaven?" If they answer, "I think so," or "I hope so," you can then ask, "Has anybody ever taken a Bible and shown you how you can know you're going to heaven?" With their permission, you must then proceed to give a clear presentation of the Gospel, inviting them to trust in Christ.

Should they respond to the initial question, "Yes, I know I'd go to heaven," you can then ask, "If you stood before God and He were to ask you, 'Why should I let you into heaven?' what would you say?" If they answer by explaining the good things they have done and the good life they have lived, you can ask, "May I show you what the Bible says about that?" and proceed to give a clear presentation of the Gospel, explaining the aspects of sin, substitution, and faith.

There Are Those Who Have Never Grasped Eternal Security

There is absolutely no one whose salvation concerns me more than the one says, "I believe in salvation by grace. I just don't believe in once saved, always saved."

The Bible is abundantly clear that once God gives the free gift of eternal life, He never takes back that gift. The two words *eternal life* in and of themselves are enough to verify that. "Eternal life" that one has one moment and loses the next is everything but eternal. God would be less than truthful if He were to say to us, "I give you eternal life upon simple trust in Christ," and then went on to say, "But please bear in mind I might recall that gift." Life that is not eternal is simply not eternal life.

The Scriptures could not be any clearer than they are that to be His, is to be His forever. John 5:24 tells us, "Most assuredly, I say to you, he who hears My word and believes in Him who sent Me *has* everlasting life, and *shall not* come into judgment, but *has passed* from death into life." John 10:28 explains, "And I give them eternal life, and they shall never perish; neither shall anyone snatch them out of My hand." The context of that latter verse is that in order to lose our salvation we would have to be greater than God Himself. He is holding us, we are not holding Him. Also, what could be clearer than Romans 11:29 where we are told, "For the gifts and the calling of God are irrevocable." Even if we change our minds about Him, He never changes His mind about us.

So, are those who do not believe in eternal security unbelievers? I am convinced there are those who I refer to as "scared but secure." They are sincerely trusting in Christ alone as their only basis for a right standing with God. But they have yet to fully comprehend the abundant love and grace He has for them.

There are also those who say, "I don't believe in once saved, always saved," who are not saying what they mean and are not expressing where they are hurting. What distresses them is the idea that a person can come to Christ and then, as they often put it, "Go out and paint the town red." The Scriptures are clear that when we come to Christ, we ought to live on a day by day basis the holiest life we can for the Savior. The desire to "Be holy, for I am holy" (1 Peter 1:16) ought to be preeminent in our minds, always recognizing that a holy life can only be lived through the power of Christ who lives within us. As Paul testified in Galatians 2:20, "I have been crucified with Christ; it is no longer I who live, but Christ lives in me; and the life which I now live in the flesh I live by faith in the Son of God, who loved me and gave Himself for me."

Although exhorted to live a holy life, God's acceptance of us is not based on our performance, it is based on His Son's performance in atoning for our sins. Even if we disappoint Him, He never disappoints us. Just as a human child can walk in disobedience to his or her human parents and dishonor them, so a child of God can walk in disobedience to the heavenly Father and dishonor Him. Such a life invites the discipline of God upon the believer (Heb. 12:5–11), but does not change the fact that to be His is to be His forever.

With that said, however, there *are* those who do not believe in eternal security who concern me. The reason is I am convinced that many of them have not comprehended the grace of God. Instead of trusting Christ to save them, they are trusting their works or even Christ *plus* their works to save them. Biblically, one is never saved until one has trusted Christ alone.

I have found the following illustration valuable in helping such a person understand the sufficiency of Christ's death on the cross.

I draw three circles. One stands for works (W), the second stands for Christ and works (C+W), and the third stands for Christ alone (C). The circles look like this:

I then explain, "Some trust their works to get them to heaven. Some trust Christ plus their works. Some trust Christ alone. Where are you?" Many who do not believe in eternal security have pointed to the C+W circle. I then state, "If you are trusting your works to save you, you are saying to God, 'Your Son's death was unnecessary.' After all, if anything we did got us to heaven, there was no need for Christ to die on a cross." I then write the word *unnecessary* below the first circle. I continue, "If you are trusting Christ plus works, you are saying to God, 'Your Son's death was disappointing.' In essence you are saying to God, 'You paid for those sins, and I'll pay for these.' Salvation then becomes a partnership, not a gift." I write the word *disappointing* below the second circle. I finish by saying, "If you are trusting Christ alone, you are saying to God, 'Your Son's death was sufficient.'" I write the word *sufficient* below the third circle. So the three circles now look like this:

I then explain that one is never saved until one has trusted Christ alone. The message of the Gospel is that we *must* be satisfied with the thing that satisfies God. God was not satisfied with our good works in any way, shape, or partial form. He was only satisfied with His Son's death on the cross. *Propitiation* in the Scriptures means "satisfaction." Referring to Jesus Christ and His death on the cross, 1 John 2:2 tells us *He Himself*, not our good works or Christ and our good works, but He Himself was the propitiation for our sins, and not for ours only but also for the sins of the whole world. It has been exciting to observe the "light" come on in the faces of so many, see them exclaim, "I see it!" and transfer their trust to Christ alone to save them.

There Are Those Who Have Been the Victims of Unbiblical Teaching

Scripture plainly says, "Be diligent to present yourself approved to God, a worker who does not need to be ashamed, rightly dividing the word of truth" (2 Tim. 2:15). Unfortunately, there are those who have not studied the Word of God accurately and carefully enough. For that reason they have taught concepts and ideas not in keeping with the Scriptures. That is not in any way to question the zeal or the love for the Lord demonstrated by the teachers. Instead, it is to express regret at the careless way the Scriptures have been handled. I am speaking of the kind of caution and accuracy needed to read out of the Bible what it is actually saying, not read into it what we'd like it to say.

What are some of those erroneous and unbiblical concepts that have been taught to others? Allow me to cite two.

"If You Don't Know the Date You Were Saved, You Are Not Saved."

There is a particular second in which each individual is transferred from the kingdom of darkness into the kingdom of light. Nowhere, though, does the Scripture teach that if you do not *know* the date, you are not saved. John 3:16 emphatically states, "For God so loved the world that He gave His only begotten Son, that whoever believes in Him should not perish but have everlasting life." It does not state, "Whoever believes in Him and *knows the date*." If you can say, "I am trusting Christ alone as my only way to heaven," you're saved regardless of when and where you crossed the line.

Multitudes know the date. Multitudes don't. I'm convinced there are multitudes that are *wrong* on the date. When they stand before the Lord, they will discover they were saved days, months, or even years before or after the date they had commonly given. God in His infinite wisdom and knowledge knows at what point in time a particular individual appropriated the grace of God. But nowhere does the Bible state that a believer has to be certain of that point. If the believer is trusting Christ alone, regardless of the date the transaction took place, he or she is forever a child of God.

This is such a comfort to those whose conversion was not as radical as others. Some had lived such a rebellious life, their conversion was like Paul's experience on the Damascus road. I could relay a multitude of these experiences of which I have been privileged to be a part. For others, their conversion was so gradual because of the slow process by which they came to understand God's simple plan of salvation, that it is more difficult for them to cite the place and the time they became His. I could also relay a multitude of those experiences as well. Either way, although there *was* a split second the divine transaction took place, as long as these people are trusting Christ alone, they are forever His.

If a person goes back to a date or an experience, he or she will *never* have assurance of salvation or, at best, will have a faulty assurance. If what one thinks happened, happened, one is saved. If what one thinks happened did not happen, one is not saved. In light of the fact that no one can relive history, one cannot be certain. The Scriptures never command us to memorize the date we are saved or go back to a particular experience but simply ask us to answer the question, "Am I trusting Christ alone to save me?" If so, the certainty of everlasting life is ours. The concept "If you don't know the date you were saved, you are not saved" is absolutely unbiblical.

"If You Don't Pray, Love, Forgive (and the list goes on and on), You Are Not Saved."

I grieve how many times I've heard statements such as:

Any bored Christian is no Christian at all.

You can pray and not be a Christian, but you cannot be a Christian and not pray.

If you don't evangelize, you are not saved.

If you cannot forgive others, you have never become a Christian.

If you have not allowed God to have control of every area of your life, you have not come to Him.

Don't misunderstand. Christians ought to pray, evangelize, forgive, demonstrate the happiness of Christian living, and allow Him to have control of their lives. But these things are part of discipleship and growth. They are never in Scripture made conditions of salvation.

A good example is found in the small epistle of 1 John. We are told in 1 John 4:20, "If someone says, 'I love God,' and hates his brother, he is a liar; for he who does not love his brother whom he has seen, how can he love God whom he has not seen?" I grieve how many times I've heard that verse used to declare, "Therefore, if you do not love your brother, you are not a Christian."

What is the problem with this kind of thinking? For one, if that is true, we have a tremendous problem with numerous texts such as 1 Corinthians 6:1–11 where believers are so unloving they are even going to court against each other. Yet Paul addresses them as "brethren" and never once doubts their salvation. The second problem is that it represents a careless handling of Scripture, interpreting it out of context instead of in context. John makes it clear he is writing his first epistle to discuss fellowship with the Father. His purpose in writing is stated in the third and fourth verses of chapter 1 where he writes, "that which we have seen and heard we declare to you, that you also may have fellowship with us; and truly our fellowship is with the Father and with His Son Jesus Christ. And these things we write to you that your joy may be full." With that in mind, the word abide is used twenty-six times. Therefore, John's purpose in writing is not to tell us how to come to Christ, but instead how to get close to Christ. That is why the Gospel of John and 1 John make such beautiful companion volumes. The Gospel of John explains how to come to Christ while 1 John explains how to abide in the One to whom we have come.

One can now see the meaning of 1 John 4:20. One can *know* God and hate his brother. How many Christians do you and I both know who have struggled in that area? However, one cannot *love* God and hate his brother. If we love the Father, we have to love His family; otherwise we cannot say, "I love God." Therefore, it is most fitting for John to continue by saying, "And this commandment we have from Him: that he who loves God must love his brother also." How absolutely essential it is for us to interpret Scripture in context!

In fact, the place where John discusses eternal salvation is in the final chapter of his epistle. Interestingly enough, the terms of the Gospel are the same as those given in the Gospel of John. He writes, "And this is the testimony: that God has given us eternal life, and this life is in His Son. He who has the Son has life; he who does not have the Son of God does not have life. These things I have written to you who believe in the name of the Son of God, that you may know that you have eternal life" (1 John 5:11–13). There is one condition for salvation—personal trust in Jesus Christ. There are many conditions for abiding—loving one another, forgiving one another, studying the Scriptures, prayer—all of which contribute to the closeness of our fellowship with the Father. But we dare not confuse fellowship and Christian growth with what is necessary to stand justified before God.

Does that mean that one who has difficulty forgiving another is not saved? That could well be the problem. But that is not the *basis* on which to determine our salvation. Who of us could say we've never struggled forgiving particular individuals? But for our own assurance and sanity we dare not confuse entering the Christian life with living the Christian life.

Because individuals have confused the *condition* for entering the Christian life with the *conditions* for living the Christian life, they have caused multitudes to be confused about their eternal salvation. When it comes to determining if we are saved we must ask and answer the simple question, "Have I placed my trust in Christ alone as my only way to heaven?" If so, we can rest in the certainty of eternal life. If we find we are not as loving, forgiving, giving, or prayerful as we should be, we can then ask, "What is hindering my Christian growth? How can I grow more as a Christian?" But we need never question whether we are His.

With that understood, how do we help individuals determine if theirs is a salvation issue or a Christian growth issue? The answer is a quite simple one—by helping *them* decide where they are. To do so, I ask, "If you were to die right now and stand before God and He were to ask you, 'Why should I let you into heaven?' what would you say?" If their answer is clear that their trust is in Jesus Christ alone, I then explain the difference between becoming a Christian and growing as a Christian and have a delightful discussion about how to grow as a believer. If their answer reveals that they do not understand the Gospel, I explain God's free gift of eternal life, help them settle that issue, and then explain how to grow as a Christian and live the kind of life I refer to as a "thank you" letter to God.

There Are Those Who Doubt Everything

Some people struggle with the assurance of their salvation because they struggle with life period. That is, they doubt just about everything. That was the situation with the woman I described in opening this chapter. As we talked, I sensed her problem was more than where she stood with God. I eventually said to her, "Let me explain something. I'm convinced your problem is far more than doubting your salvation. I think you doubt everything. For example, do you have any doubts your husband loves you?" As she wept, she immediately told me of her struggles in that area. I then continued, "Do you have any doubts that your children love you?" She told me of her doubts in that area as well.

Such people are usually in need of professional and long-term counseling to get their thinking in order. Their struggle over salvation is only a symptom. The problem is often deeply rooted in parental abuse, spousal abuse, a low self-image, feelings of betrayal, and a host of other things. I have even met those who struggle over their salvation because they have never experienced the consistent love of a human father. They wrestle at times with how God could consistently love them as well. Biblical and long-term counseling often helps these individuals come to a point where God's thinking and their thinking—as it relates to life, others, themselves, and the promises of God's Word—are the same. They can then relax in the thought that what God has forever settled in His mind can be settled in theirs. Jesus said, "He who believes in Me has everlasting life," (John 6:47) and that settles it.

Conclusion

"He is saved. He just lacks assurance." If I have heard that comment once, I've heard it a thousand times. But as I have studied the Scripture, I've been forced to exclaim, "Wait a minute. What do you mean?" After all, security or assurance is part and parcel of the offer. God is not just promising eternal life upon trusting Christ. He is promising the *certainty* of eternal life. First John 5:13 does not say, "These things I have written to you who believe in the name of the Son of God, that you might *think* that you have eternal life." It says that you may *know* you have eternal life. If there is no assurance, where is the certainty?

The reason some people suffer lack of assurance can only be determined through one means—interaction—asking the right questions and giving them the opportunity to respond. One thing is for certain: The time and patience needed to help them is worth it all if they come to that point of knowing that heaven is their future destination. Although many things in life might well change, and life can end abruptly, they can relax in the thought that the day of their death will be better than the day of their birth. This is unquestionably the most relaxing way to live, resting in the assurance of the Lord's salvation.

QUESTIONS FOR REFLECTION

- Why is asking the right questions so imperative to finding out if a person understands God's simple plan of salvation?

- In what ways should the beauty and meaning of Christ's words "It is finished" motivate us to live our lives for the Savior?

- Why is it important to examine everything we hear by the clear teachings of Scripture?

- Can you think of ways other than those mentioned in this chapter that the field of evangelism has been plagued by false concepts and ideas?

- What are other ways we so easily confuse entering the Christian life with living the Christian life?

Chapter Thirteen

How to Help Your Church
Get on the Cutting Edge
in Evangelism . . . and Stay There

ↄ₰₽

I could not wait to meet him. Hearing non-Christians and Christians alike talk about him, you would have thought Jesus Christ Himself had walked through the town. Although now retired, this town's pastor of over fifty years had so impacted people that lost people had been brought to Christ, families reunited, and godly households established. Respecting what the Book of Proverbs says about the wisdom of men who have both age and experience, I had one particular question I wanted to ask him.

My opportunity came one afternoon as we sat and talked together. "You were a pastor in this town for over fifty years. Not only your church but the whole town has felt the impact of your ministry," I said. "When you look at the church as a whole, where it was fifty years ago and where it is today, what do you see as the difference?" His ready reply told me he had often asked and answered that himself. "The lack of prayer and the lack of evangelism," he said. "The church that existed fifty years ago was a praying church and an evangelizing church. The church today is neither."

Fortunately, that is not always the case. But it is more true than we often want to admit. So much has the church lost its cutting edge in evangelism that a denominational leader observed, "We have become keepers of the aquarium instead of fishers of men." Search as we may, we are hard pressed to find a church that grows by conversion instead of by transfer of believers from one church to another. As one pastor lamented, "We are in the Christian relocation business. What we are doing is transferring Christians from one church to another."

Why has the church lost its cutting edge in evangelism? Can it be regained?

There is no question that the cutting edge can be regained. The God whose heart bleeds for the lost is still on the throne. Understanding, though, why we have lost the cutting edge can be a huge step in regaining it. Properly analyzing a problem always helps in arriving at a solution. Having a son myself, I am amused by the story of the boy who refused to take his little sister along to fish in the pond nearby. He protested to his mother, "The last time she went with me, I could not catch a single fish." The mother promised, "Look, I'll talk to her, and I promise you this time she won't make any noise." The brother answered, "It wasn't the noise, Mom—she ate all the bait!" In any situation, properly analyzing the problem is a big help.

Recognizing the cutting edge, though, is not the job of the church leaders and it's not the job of the laypeople. Instead, it's the job of both. The leaders can't do it without the help of the laypeople, and the laypeople can't do it without the assistance of the leaders. With that in mind, what can they both do to put their church back on track and see it make a genuine impact in evangelizing a community for Christ?

Recognize the Need for Balance

By nature we are people of extremes. We are either stingy or spendthrift. We either treat our family like they don't matter or we treat them like they are the only thing in life that does matter. *Balance* has always been easier to pronounce than practice. Years ago church leaders began to realize the dearth of good Bible teaching. They realized the need for solid Bible teaching from the pulpit. Bible churches began springing up across the country, and the ability to be an expository preacher became a "test" of the call to the ministry. But teaching became the emphasis, to the exclusion of evangelism. The pendulum swung not to the middle but to the other side. One pastor agonized to me, "We've missed the point of Mark 10:45: 'The Son of Man did not come to be served, but to serve.' The mentality of individuals coming to church is often, 'What do you have to teach me today?'"

It's exciting to see churches changing that trend. Are they throwing out the teaching? Not for a moment. They are realizing the need to teach *and* reach.

Recognizing that I speak in a lot of churches every year and meet a lot of pastors, a search committee recently wrote to me and said, "We are looking for a pastor. Do you have anyone to suggest? We want one who is committed to exposition, but also one committed to evangelism. We are convinced there needs to be a balance." Their concern was understandable. The Great Commission of Matthew 28:19–20 is not "Go and *transfer* disciples" but "Go and *make* disciples." Furthermore, a church quickly dries up if the same people come every Sunday, even if Christians come from other churches. There must be an influx of new converts. *They* are the ones who help keep a church revitalized and on target. Part of the reason is their enthusiasm.

Whenever I lead people to Christ I encourage them to tell two people that same day what has happened. I find it cements in their mind what they've done and helps them start doing what they ought to do the rest of their lives—tell others. On numerous occasions I've had them look at me and say something such as, "Oh, don't worry. I'd like to tell two hundred."

What kind of encouragement are you to your pastor? Do you give him the distinct impression that you come to "sit, soak, and sour" and that as long as he gives you a morsel of truth to take home with you, you are completely satisfied? Or do you let him know that you would welcome messages from time to time directed to non-Christians— messages you can invite *your* non-Christian friends to hear? Do you by your own *example* and *encouragement* assure him that you wish to see your church teach but you also wish to see it reach? What about the balance in your own life? Do you simply spend your life with Christians or do you spend it with non-Christians as well—ones whom you might reach for the Savior?

I was in the home of a couple who feel that the reason God has them at their present address is because He wants to use their home as a "mission station" to evangelize the community. They love the Word and are the type of people every pastor loves to have in his church. But they also love the lost. They participate in sports with non-Christians, have them in their home for dinner, and do business with them. I can tell you from firsthand observation that they have played a tremendous part in keeping the church balanced through the balance in their own lives.

Help Lighten the Load—Don't Add to It

Consider another factor that causes a church to lose its cutting edge. The average Christian home today is so plagued by problems and anxieties that a businessman remarked, "I have so many worries that if something else came along to worry about, it would be tomorrow before I could get to it." Ask Christians to list their concerns and among the top items on the list would be: raising children, maintaining a good marriage, financial pressures, job insecurity, and the possibility of cancer.

So much attention is given to the problems of believers that the lost fall by the wayside. An experienced church leader will admit that if a church is to be evangelistic, the leader is the key. If evangelism is not caught from him by example, it won't be taught to his people through exhortation. But pastors and church leaders can become so tied up counseling Christians how to get from Monday to Friday, little time is left to tell a lost person how to get from earth to heaven. A pastor of a large church in Tennessee remarked to me, "I know I need to be spending more time with the lost, but how in the world do I do that when counseling believers in my church and meeting with my staff takes so much time. There is no time left for lost people."

As a layperson, are you on your pastor's back, or are you on his team? Is your focus inward or outward? Do you become so enmeshed in your own problems and struggles that you fail to see the even greater struggles and problems of those who don't know the Lord and hence don't have the divine assistance to call on as you do?

There is something about looking at the problems of another, particularly those of a lost person or a new convert, that helps me look more objectively at my own struggles. The story is told of a doctor who asked a group of his patients, who had what they considered overwhelming health problems, to come to his office. When they arrived, he had them sit in a circle. Then he said to person number one, "I would like for you to take person number two's problem." Looking at person number two, he said, "I would like you to take person number three's problem," and continued around the circle, assigning to each person the problem of the next. After looking at the problems of the other person, they were more than delighted to keep their own! Similarly, the pastor of a large church in Oklahoma said, "I'm convinced that evangelism will take care of many problems a church has. You have more people to assist in church activities, more funds to work with . . ." and his list continued. He then added, "I have found even our people's problems have become less significant when they look at the problems of a new convert."

Are you contributing to your pastor's counseling load by not spending the time needed in prayer and Bible study so that you can receive the spiritual nourishment needed to live for Christ in today's world? An experienced pastor once shared with me, "What frustrates me about counseling is that so many of the people who come to me wouldn't be having their struggles if they had done what the Word said years ago. Now they want me to place a band-aid on a spot where there should have been major surgery."

Be Open to Change

Another reason the church has lost its cutting edge is that we have not kept in step with the times. We are living in what some church leaders call a "post-Christian" era. I have personally seen the results of that. In the seventies as I traveled as an evangelistic speaker and asked non-Christians, "Have you ever heard of John 3:16?" the standard answer was yes. If I started quoting the verse, they could often finish it. Now, the standard answer is no. So much so, I rarely use that question anymore. They have not read the Bible, talked the Christian language, or sung Christian hymns. For that reason, the question many believers are asking is, "How do I witness to people who don't accept the basic suppositions that there is one God, one Bible, and one way to heaven?"

Surveys reveal that although non-Christians have not given up on God, some have given up on the church. They feel it is no longer relevant to life. The senior pastor of a New Jersey church agonized with me about the difference in ministry today versus just ten years ago: "A few Sunday nights ago, I was late getting to the evening service. I was really disheartened when I passed a video rental store and saw one of our families coming out of it with a video they were apparently planning to watch that evening. They must have felt that was more interesting than anything going on at church." If that was true for a believer, would it not be even more true for a non-Christian?

Does that mean we change the Bible, our language, and hymns? Certainly not the Bible, and not necessarily our language or all of our hymns. Does it mean we should change the thrust for our Sunday morning service and target non-Christians? Even many church leaders who are seeing good things happen in terms of evangelism would answer no. What it does mean is that we have to be sure we are *communicating* with non-Christians and being *sensitive* to where they are coming from. The issue is not being seeker targeted, the issue is being seeker sensitive. More than ever when we plan services, we need to ask, "If a newcomer came this morning, is what we are saying and doing something they could understand and be helped by?" Remember, we are talking about the newcomer of the nineties, not the newcomer of fifty years ago. Otherwise, we may be talking but they may not be listening, and if they are listening, they might not understand the point we are making. It makes little or no sense to them.

That is why church leaders are feeling some of the greatest pressures they have ever felt. As a pastor in Pennsylvania said to me, "I know there are areas we need to change. Our people really resist any substantial change. But I get the impression if we don't make what we are doing from eleven o'clock to twelve o'clock on Sunday morning more meaningful to those who have grown up in a post-Christian era, we as a church are not even going to be here ten years from now."

How open are you as a layperson to change? Do you resist it or welcome it? Are you open to the fact that the music and service format that God used to touch your life forty years ago is not necessarily what He'll use to touch somebody else's life today? Whenever new ideas are presented, do your leaders dread a phone call from you, or do you greet those ideas with an ear willing to listen? A pastor of a church that is one hundred and fifty years old said to me, "An elderly woman in our church gets greatly upset if she sees somebody talking in the auditorium before the service. She feels that should be a quiet reverent time of preparing yourself for worship. What she doesn't understand is that we have people starting to come who don't even know what worship is. They have not had a church background."

None of us would want to admit to being hung up on tradition. But isn't tradition harder to break than we say it is? It's often helpful to approach the Scriptures by saying, "Suppose we had no experience to draw from. What do the Scriptures tell us about how to conduct our church services, programs, and activities?" Recognizing where freedom is given and is not given in Scripture can often be guiding and freeing at the same time.

Ask the Right Question

The fear of asking questions that can be intimidating is another reason we've lost the cutting edge. Based on the Great Commission of Matthew 28:19–20, one question church leaders need to ask at the end of every year is, "How many people have been brought to Christ by the collective witness of our church and are now being discipled to become growing Christians?" Ouch! Does that question ever hurt! It is far easier to ask, "How many new families have been added to our church this year?" and overlook the fact that ninety percent of them were already believers when they came through our doors.

Years ago, before going into full-time evangelism, I pastored a church close to Baltimore, Maryland. In terms of growth, we saw exciting things happen. But every month we had to resist the temptation of asking, "How many more people are here this month than last month?" We had to continually force ourselves to ask, "How many are joining our church through conversion?" Only then can we get a realistic (and biblical) view of the difference we were making.

I spoke at a church in Florida that was bursting at the seams—so much so they needed to develop a building program. The leaders were excited, the people were excited—everyone was excited. Who wouldn't be! It is more exciting being part of a growing church than a dying church. I met with the pastor, though, and found him the least excited of all. I asked why and he told me, "Two churches in the community are having problems, so all we are doing is getting the people who are leaving those churches. Somehow that doesn't seem to be what the Great Commission is all about." Now imagine what would happen if the leaders in a spirit of objectivity and support for each other would sit down and ask, "How many people who have been brought to Christ by our church are now being discipled to be growing Christians?" The answer would be disappointing, but it would keep the church from reveling in how many were coming as Christians, instead of examining the impact they were having on the lost.

How much pressure do you as a layperson put on your leaders in this area? If they want to grow by conversion not by transfer, are you on their support team, or do you far too often raise the question, "Why are other churches in this town growing and we aren't?" That might be a good question. But be careful to recognize how they are growing—transfer or conversion—before you become too critical of your own leadership. They might have the courage to examine something other churches are not examining.

Satan Is Alive and Well— But So Is Prayer

Whatever we do in evaluating why the church has lost its cutting edge in evangelism, we dare not underestimate Satan. A seminary professor once said, "You always need to ask, 'If you were the Devil, how would you keep the church from reaching the lost?'" If I were Satan, I would engage in getting a church messed up—Christian husbands and wives divorcing each other, petty arguments within the church, and doing everything I could to trip church leaders up in sin—all of which is rampant today. As a result, Christians are known for their testimony, but it's often a bad one instead of a good one. Non-Christians often see the church as a place where people fight instead of fellowship.

Three boys were one time talking about the occupations and abilities of their dads. One boy said, "My dad's a doctor and he practices medicine." The second said, "My dad's an attorney and he practices law." The third remarked, "My dad's a Christian but he's not practicing right now." That's why, going back to the pastors comment I began with, the church needs to be a praying church—praying about the witness we have with both our lips and our life. Daily we need to ask God to take out of our lives what should not be there and put in what should be there. It may be trite but it's also true—Satan trembles when he sees even the weakest Christian on his or her knees. Prayer has such an inherent power that it makes even the Devil tremble. The more we pray and then act upon God's leading, the better position we are in to evangelize and help keep our church on track as well.

Conclusion

I meet a lot of discouraged pastors. So when I met one recently who was elated with how things were going, I was curious. I asked, "What excites you about your ministry?" He answered, "You'll see when you are here speaking. We have a lot of new Christians in our assembly. The church has turned around a lot in the last couple of years." I wanted to encourage other pastors with whatever he was doing, so I asked, "How did you turn things around?" The first thing he mentioned was a retreat the church leaders went on where, in the spirit of harmony, they wrestled with the deeper issues of church ministry I have just addressed. They took an honest, objective, factual look at all areas of church ministry. They came away encouraged—not discouraged. One by one, they carefully examined the church from the position of a person living where all of us are now living—in a post-Christian era. Together they established some very meaningful one- to five-year goals. The changes they are making are producing a church deeply committed to the Scriptures and how to make them extremely relevant to the culture in which they are being communicated.

I got even more excited when I talked to the people. One of them said, "The church for years has been known as a teaching station. We've done nothing in evangelism. Our leadership is really changing things around." I saw in him and many others, laypeople who are a breath of springtime to leadership—willing to be led in the right direction. Almost without exception, every time I spoke to the laypeople, they commended their leadership. And every time I spoke to the leadership, they commended the laypeople.

Pulling in the same direction makes a phenomenal difference. If you're a layperson, you need the help of your leadership to bring your church to the cutting edge of evangelism. But remember, the leaders need your help as well.

QUESTIONS FOR REFLECTION

- How much time within the last six months have you spent in meaningful contact and conversations with the lost?

- In what specific ways within the next six months do you plan to be an encouragement to your church leaders in helping them build a church that impacts the community for Christ?

- When the church leaders think in terms of changes needed within their church, would they think of you as a person open to change or resistant to change?

- How is the ability and integrity it takes to ask the right questions essential in determining the impact your church is making in the community?

- If you were the Devil and wanted to destroy your church, how specifically would you do it?

About EvanTell

Declaring the Gospel, clearly and simply
Activating believers around the world
Preparing the next generation to reach the lost

W e're passionate about the lost—and reaching them with the gospel. Our programs help believers confidently communicate the gospel— Jesus Christ died for your sins and rose from the dead. EvanTell's ministry outreaches, evangelistic resources, live training workshops, video training curriculum and follow-up materials are built on years of evangelistic experience. Founded in 1973, the ministry was started by Dr. R. Larry Moyer out of a commitment and desire to see the gospel clearly presented with a careful handling of Scripture and a core doctrine of grace.

The Gospel. Clear and Simple.®

EvanTell, Inc.
P.O. Box 741417
Dallas, TX 75374
800.947.7359
www.evantell.org